Asleep in Christ

Helaine Burch

ISBN: 978-1-78364-478-0

THE OPEN BIBLE TRUST
Fordland Mount, Upper Basildon,
Reading, RG8 8LU, UK.

www.obt.org.uk

Contents

*****

Introduction

The following is a study aid which encourages serious inquiry into the nature of mankind and his destiny after death. It is written with the affirmation that the Bible is the inspired Word of God, and as such is unerring in its truth and complete in its teaching. For many hundreds of years, each generation has interpreted the Scriptures with the viewpoint handed down to them by their forbears. The eternal nature of man has long been considered a given, though the Bible itself does not specifically address or confirm the belief. The purpose of this study is to examine the Scriptures with an open mind to discover what they actually do reveal about life and death.

In order to allow the Bible to speak for itself as much as possible, we shall avoid interpreting with a doctrinal vocabulary which does not find its source within the word of God. If our understanding is to be based solely on Biblical teaching - which it should be - then we will not want to rely on unscriptural terminology to explain the basics of man's existence. To aid the reader in identifying the most common unscriptural terms, please take note of the list below which presents expressions and phrases which *do not* occur in the Scriptures:

immortal soul	eternal soul
immortal spirit	spiritual death
immortality of the soul	physical death
immortality of the spirit	eternal hell
separated soul	eternal conscious torment
separated spirit	eternal conscious punishment
disembodied soul	eternal separation from God
disembodied spirit	purgatory
intermediate state	limbo

There is no harm in using an unscriptural expression when describing an established concept, as long as it does not act to distort or alter the concept itself. A case in point would be the "Trinity," a word which accurately represents the complex nature of the godhead. But if we use the above terms to describe doctrine and freely interpolate them into our Bible readings, there may be a danger of departing from the intended concepts of Scripture. When we read and think "eternal soul" while the Bible says only "soul," we are adding a defining word which may ultimately influence the way we perceive the "soul." We might also note that the very popular terms listed above seem quite essential to our modern-day teachers, and yet they were never even used by the writers of the Bible. This is something we should all be concerned about, for the addition of unscriptural terminology to clarify a passage may in actuality be working to confuse the Bible's meaning.

With these things in mind, we shall endeavour to explore the Biblical teachings on life and death using the simple words and ideas which the Lord Himself has provided us through His servants. We can expect our God, as Creator, to be the very Master of reasoning, and to present us with a perfect and logical set of Scriptures. In them are no mistakes and no inconsistencies beyond that which is the result of human interpretation and translation. All of His word fits together flawlessly, and if we think we see a flaw, it is in our own thinking - not His.

1. What is death – according to the Bible?

When we examine the Scriptures with the aim of establishing a Biblical definition of death, we will find the demise of man described in straightforward statements that are easily understood. Rather than implying a continuing existence that is characterized by consciousness, the passages presented here give evidence that man is silent and senseless when he joins the ranks of "the dead."

> For the living know that they shall die: but the dead know not any thing, neither have they any more a reward; for the memory of them is forgotten. Also their love, and their hatred, and their envy, is now perished; neither have they any more a portion for ever in any thing that is done under the sun ... Whatsoever thy hand findeth to do, do it with thy might; for there is no work, nor device, nor knowledge, nor wisdom, in the grave, whither thou goest. (Ecclesiastes 9:5-6,10)

According to Solomon, knowledge, memory, and emotion perish in death. The living are said to be aware, for they "know" that they shall die, but the dead are not in possession of any such awareness. Since they "know not any thing," it is very unlikely that they can have self-consciousness or perception. Note also that the passage does not attribute this lack of awareness to dead *bodies*, but to "the dead," a term which plainly indicates those people who have died. Thus, it would seem that all the powers of the mind are lost when death occurs, as the psalmist also testifies in the passage given below:

> Put not your trust in princes, nor in the son of man, in whom there is no help. His breath goeth forth, he returneth to his earth; in that very day his thoughts perish. (Psalm 146:3-4)

Read all of Psalm 146 and note how the short life of man is contrasted with the eternal nature of the Lord. While man returns to his earth and his thoughts perish with him, the Lord is said to be "forever" (verse 10), and His reign shall never cease. When it comes to the nature of the life within him and the duration of his existence, it appears that man far more resembles the animals than he does his eternal God.

Man being in honour abideth not: he is like the beasts that perish ... Like sheep they are laid in the grave; death shall feed on them; and the upright shall have dominion over them in the morning; and their beauty shall consume in the grave from their dwelling. (Psalm 49:12,14)

Man's nature is said to be identical to that of the beasts; he does not "abide" forever, but perishes in his death. In the next passage, from Job, note how a comparison is used to reinforce the teaching that is set before us:

For there is hope of a tree, if it be cut down, that it will sprout again, and that the tender branch thereof will not cease. Though the root thereof wax old in the earth, and the stock thereof die in the ground; yet through the scent of water it will bud, and bring forth boughs like a plant. But man dieth, and wasteth away: yea, man giveth up the ghost, and where is he? As the waters fail from the sea, and the flood decayeth and drieth up: so man lieth down, and riseth not: till the heavens be no more, they shall not awake, nor be raised out of their sleep. (Job 14:7-12)

When a tree is cut down, there is still hope that it may sprout again, and that it is not truly dead - but "man dieth, and wasteth away." There is no hope that life remains within him, and no hope that he will spontaneously "sprout" once again. Job compares the death of man to evaporated flood waters, an analogy which suggests that he is simply gone. The verses do not indicate that man continues to live on after the death of the body; but rather, the question "where is he?" implies the opposite, that he has come to a full and complete end. Job gives additional information about death when he speaks despondently to his friends in chapter 17:

If I wait, the grave is mine house: I have made my bed in the darkness. I have said to corruption, 'Thou art my father:' to the worm, 'Thou art my mother, and my sister.' And where is now my hope? as for my hope, who shall see it? They shall go down to the bars of the pit, when our rest together is in the dust. (Job 17:13-16)

Here Job speaks of "making his bed" in the darkness, a figure which suggests that nothing can be seen in the sleep-like state of death. He also implies that his "hope" will disappear when he dies, and rest with him in the grave; he will not be consciously waiting and hoping for events that will take place in the future. See also Job 10:21-22, where death is called "the land of darkness," and a shadow "without any order." These metaphors are in good harmony with the words of Heman below, showing that Job's view of death is right on the mark.

> Shall Thy loving-kindness be declared in the grave? Or Thy faithfulness in destruction? Shall Thy wonders be known in the dark? And Thy righteousness in the land of forgetfulness? (Psalm 88:11-12)

It is apparent that Heman meant these rhetorical questions to receive a "no" answer, and they therefore paint us a vivid picture of man's future. The verses establish "the grave" as a place of destruction ... the place where each man comes to an end. Death is figuratively called "the land of forgetfulness" because the brain ceases to operate once it has been destroyed through decomposition. The Lord's loving-kindness, wonders, faithfulness, and righteousness cannot be known in the grave, for man "forgets" everything when he sleeps the dark sleep of death.

> Return, O Lord, deliver my soul: Oh save me for Thy mercies' sake. For in death there is no remembrance of Thee: in the grave who shall give Thee thanks? (Psalm 6:4-5)

Because the dead "know not anything" (Ecclesiastes 9:5), they consequently cannot remember the Lord, neither can they praise Him or offer thanksgiving. Here David asks to be delivered out of the hands of his enemies, for he knows that in death there is no way to worship his God. Psalm 30 below is in full agreement, for the writer implies through rhetorical questioning that, once dead, he is no longer profitable to the Lord.

> What profit is there in my blood, when I go down to the pit? Shall the dust praise Thee? Shall it declare Thy truth? (Psalm 30:9)

When a man goes down to the grave in death, all that remains is dust, which is incapable of a relationship with God. This concept is very different from the traditional view that man can continue his fellowship with God after death. The inability to communicate is confirmed in even plainer words in Psalm 115:17

> The dead praise not the Lord, neither any that go down into silence. (Psalm 115:17)

Those who have died go down into the silence of the grave ... they cannot speak. Thus a man can only praise the Lord and declare His truth when he is alive.

> Praise ye the Lord. Praise the Lord, O my soul. While I live will I praise the Lord: I will sing praises unto my God while I have any being. (Psalm 146:1-2)

The psalmist says here that he will praise the Lord while he lives, "while I have any being." These words suggest that he will no longer praise the Lord when he dies, and that there will come a time when he no longer has "any being." The psalmist therefore does not appear to view himself as eternal, but instead implies that he expects to come to an end. See also Psalm 116:2 where the psalmist says, "I will call upon Him as long as I live." Again the implication is that there will come a time when he no longer lives, and no longer can call. The writers of Scripture make it quite clear that when death comes upon a man, he is no longer existent:

> And why dost Thou not pardon my transgression, and take away mine iniquity? for now shall I sleep in the dust; and Thou shalt seek me in the morning, but I shall not be. (Job 7:21)

Here Job speaks of his death, and uses the figure of "sleeping in the dust." The latter half of the verse indicates that while he is sleeping he "shall not be," and even the Lord will not be able to find him. Again we see that in death the lines of communication are severed between man and his Creator.

> For the grave cannot praise Thee, death cannot celebrate Thee: they that go down into the pit cannot hope for Thy truth. The living, the living, he shall praise Thee, as I do this day: the father to the children shall make known Thy truth. (Isaiah 38:18-19)

The words of Hezekiah, who "had been sick, and was recovered of his sickness" (verse 9), powerfully demonstrate that the dead have no consciousness of the Lord God. Those who have died cannot rejoice in Him, and they are not even able to hope for His truth. Thus, Hezekiah expressed gladness in that he had recovered and was alive: "The living, the living, *he* shall praise Thee." Only the living are capable of knowing and worshipping God.

Given these testimonies, read plainly and without additions, it does not seem possible that man dies and yet continues to exist in a state of full self-awareness. The Scriptures teach that man is senseless, thoughtless, and without memory after death. And more significantly, these verses indicate that in death there is no relationship to be shared between man and his God. The deceased become silent and rest in the dust, unable to communicate with God, to receive His light, or to experience the joy - or misery - that is traditionally attributed to the dead.

Unfortunately, it is true that many of the Scriptures which illustrate this concept have been designated as "human reasonings" by some of history's more modern theologians. It has been suggested that the ancients were not fully enlightened about what happened after death, and that the words of Solomon, for instance, depict his false conception of what death is like. But at the close of Ecclesiastes, Solomon asserted that his writings were "upright, even words of truth" (12:10). It is difficult to imagine that God would give this man the gift of wisdom (1 Kings 4:29-34) and inspire him to write a portion of the Holy Scriptures, only to have him write down his own erroneous guesses and reasonings. We should also remember that the ancients lived at a time when God talked to men, both personally and through His prophets. To dismiss their straightforward teachings as the words of ignorant men would be to lay aside Scripture that is rich with their distinctive insights.

The death of man, then, can be defined as the end of his life, an event which brings about the total cessation of all vital functions. This would include not only the heart and lungs, but especially the brain, which is undoubtedly the most marvelous organ that he possesses. The brain has the amazing capacity to receive and interpret stimuli from every corner of the body, and in this manner it is responsible for bestowing sight, hearing, taste, smell, and touch, (the latter of which conveys the ability to feel pain and pleasure). The brain also controls both voluntary and involuntary actions, and is the seat of thought, emotion, and self-awareness. When this precious organ is stopped through death and decomposition, all of its activities cease and the man comes to "silence," "darkness," "destruction," and "dust."

Traditionally, however, most of the brain's faculties have been attributed to the "eternal soul" of an individual, and thus the senses are alleged to continue on after death, enabling the eternal personality to experience total awareness. But it is not very reasonable to allow that the dead can continue to see without eyes, hear without ears, feel without nerves, or think without a brain. We must question how they could have these abilities - as well as thought, emotion, or self-awareness - while they are totally bereft of their senses and isolated within a state of disembodiment. Without a body and its brain, a man has lost that apparatus which is crucial for living. When he is dead he can no longer function in any way, and he must have another body provided if he is ever to live again.

When we see by the Scriptures that man is so completely dissolved and disabled by death, it is logical to conclude that he cannot be inherently *immortal*. This appears to be confirmed by the passage below, in which the Apostle Paul makes reference to the Lord Jesus Christ:

> The King of kings, and Lord of lords; Who only hath immortality, dwelling in the light which no man can approach unto; Whom no man hath seen, nor can see: to Whom be honour and power everlasting. (1 Timothy 6:15-16)

The apostle has declared Jesus Christ to be the only One possessing immortality. It follows that no man can approach or see the Lord, for the death of a mortal man brings him not to Christ's dwelling place, but to the dust of the grave. No man who is now living on the earth and no man who has "passed away" possesses the eternal deathlessness of immortality. Only Christ, by means of His resurrection into a new spiritual body, is alive forever beyond the grave.

So we see that man, at this moment, is still a mortal and corruptible being. He is fully subject to death and decomposition, and will remain so until that future day when God chooses to open the graves and quicken His people. Thus, in this next passage from the great resurrection chapter of 1 Corinthians, we learn that mortal man must one day "put on" immortality in order to overcome the enemy known as death.

> The trumpet shall sound, and the dead shall be raised incorruptible, and we shall be changed. For this corruptible must put on incorruption, and this mortal must put on immortality. So when this corruptible shall have put on incorruption, and this mortal shall have put on immortality, then

shall be brought to pass the saying that is written, "Death is swallowed up in victory." (1 Corinthians 15:52-54)

If a man must "put on" immortality one day in the future, it is certain that he cannot be an immortal being at birth. Paul refers to man as "this mortal," and there is nothing in his words to suggest that man might possess an additional identity which is inherently immortal. The Scriptures do tell us that man is subject to the loss of life, at which time memory, emotion and thought perish. When we "put on" our immortality at the sounding of the last trump, only then can we say that we have had the victory over this death, for only then will we be alive again and forever unable to lose that life.

The Bible also makes it apparent that man is not born as an *eternal* being, for the word "eternal" signifies a perpetual and everlasting existence. Scripturally speaking, "eternal" is a word that is attributed to our God and to the future "eternal life" promised to the redeemed, but it is never used of man to convey an inborn nature. A quick look at a concordance will confirm this, making it quite incorrect to refer to man as eternal until the day he receives the gift of eternal life in resurrection. In the following passage, from Romans, Paul indicates that a man must *seek* for eternal life, a concept which implies that he does not now possess it:

> God; Who will render to every man according to his deeds: to them who by patient continuance in well doing seek for glory and honour and immortality, eternal life. (Romans 2:5-7)

Since the apostle has stated that immortality and eternal life must be sought for, we can allow that his doctrine is in full harmony with that of the Old Testament writers in regard to the mortal nature of man. For if the dead "go down into silence"..... if man returns to his earth and "in that very day his thoughts perish"... and if he truly "shall not be" when he has died, then indeed he must seek for resurrection to eternal life if he is ever to score a victory over death.

When we acknowledge that man is born neither immortal nor eternal, and that he is fully subject to a true and complete death, we can readily see that the privilege of living forever is a precious "gift" (Romans 6:23) to be obtained from God by those who seek it of Him through faith. This was known by the Jews when Jesus Christ came to the earth, for why else would they ask Him, "What shall I do, *that I may have* eternal life?" (Matthew 19:16).

The Bible speaks of eternal life as something given in exchange for faith (John 10:27-28) ... something hoped for (Titus 3:7) and sought for (Romans 2:7) ... something grasped for and laid hold on (1 Timothy 6:12,19). For the faithful man, eternal life is promised (2 Timothy 1:1, Hebrews 9:15, 1 John 2:24-25), but it is not yet fulfilled. It can only be realized through resurrection in the world to come (Mark 10:30).

2. Why does man die?

Having established that man ceases to live after his death, our next thought may be to ask why he dies. After all, once a man is alive, why should it ever be necessary for his life to end? The source of the earliest information to be found on the subject of death is in the book of Genesis. A detailed examination of pertinent events in the Garden of Eden will demonstrate that man's loss of life is intimately connected with his fall into sin.

> And out of the ground made the Lord God to grow every tree that is pleasant to the sight, and good for food; the tree of life also in the midst of the garden, and the tree of knowledge of good and evil ... And the Lord God commanded the man, saying, "Of every tree of the garden thou mayest freely eat: but of the tree of the knowledge of good and evil, thou shalt not eat of it: for in the day that thou eatest thereof thou shalt surely die." (Genesis 2:9, 16-17)

Adam was commanded to eat freely of all the trees, but forbidden to eat of the tree of knowledge of good and evil. Additionally, he was warned that "in the day that thou eatest thereof thou shalt surely die." In the Hebrew, the words are "dying you will die," and are very emphatic. The expression is used repeatedly in the Old Testament to forewarn the natural and visible death of various men (Genesis 20:7, 1 Samuel 22:16, 2 Kings 1:4, Jeremiah 26:8).

> Now the serpent was more subtil than any beast of the field which the Lord God had made. And he said unto the woman, "Yea, hath God said, 'Ye shall not eat of every tree of the garden'?" And the woman said unto the serpent, "We may eat of the fruit of the trees of the garden; but of the fruit of the tree which is in the midst of the garden, God hath said, 'Ye shall not eat of it, neither shall ye touch it, lest ye die.'" And the serpent said unto the woman, "Ye shall not surely die: for God doth know that in the day ye eat thereof, then your eyes shall be opened, and ye shall be as gods, knowing good and evil." And when the woman saw that the tree was good for food, and that it was pleasant to the eyes, and a tree to be desired to make one wise, she took of the fruit thereof, and did eat, and gave also unto her husband with her; and he did eat. And the eyes of them both were opened, and they knew that they were naked; and they sewed fig leaves together, and made themselves aprons. And they heard the voice of the Lord God walking in the garden in the cool of the day: and Adam and his wife hid themselves from the presence of the Lord God amongst the trees of the garden. (Genesis 3:1-8)

In trying to convince Eve to eat the forbidden fruit, Satan attempted to make God seem a liar by contradicting His words with a lie of his own: "Ye shall not surely die." Eve was deceived, and eventually both she and her husband ate, committing the sin of disobedience to God's law. Adam and Eve then became aware of their nakedness, and probably experienced guilt as well as shame. They attempted to cover themselves and hide within the garden, but God sought them out and pronounced His judgment on their deed.

> Unto the woman He said, "I will greatly multiply thy sorrow and thy conception; in sorrow thou shalt bring forth children; and thy desire shall be to thy husband, and he shall rule over thee." And unto Adam He said, "Because thou hast hearkened unto the voice of thy wife, and hast eaten of the tree, of which I commanded thee saying, 'Thou shalt not eat of it:' cursed is the ground for thy sake; in sorrow shalt thou eat of it all the days of thy life; thorns also and thistles shall it bring forth to thee; and thou shalt eat the herb of the field; in the sweat of thy face shalt thou eat bread, till thou return unto the ground; for out of it wast thou taken: for dust thou art, and unto dust shalt thou return." (Genesis 3:16-19)

Adam and Eve were no longer to live the easy life of paradise, but would now have to fend for themselves in a world made hostile with thorns and thistles. They would work and sweat for a living, and then they would return to the ground out of which they were taken: "For dust thou art, and unto dust shalt thou return." These solemn words are God's declaration of the nature of man, and with it, His pronouncement of Adam and Eve's death sentence. Note that there is no mention or hint of eternal conscious punishment as a result of man's fall into sin. Rather, the fate that God speaks of is the one that would later be described in the first Hallelujah Psalm: "His breath goeth forth, *he returneth to his earth*; in that very day his thoughts perish" (Psalm 146:4).

> Unto Adam also and to his wife did the Lord God make coats of skins, and clothed them. And the Lord God said, "Behold, the man is become as one of Us, to know good and evil: and now, lest he put forth his hand, and take also of the tree of life, and eat, and live for ever." Therefore the Lord God sent him forth from the garden of Eden, to till the ground from whence he was taken. So He drove out the man; and He placed Cherubim, and a flaming sword which turned every way, to keep the way of the tree of life. (Genesis 3:21-24)

It is apparent from this last passage that in order to "live forever," Adam and Eve had to eat of the tree of life. The Lord God drove them out of the garden specifically to prevent them from partaking of the tree, and He posted guards to ensure that they would not gain access. It is logical to conclude that without the tree of life, Adam and Eve could not live forever, nor could any of their descendants. The expulsion from the garden was thus enacted to make certain that man would indeed return to the dust.

Before the expulsion took place, however, Adam and Eve had free access to the tree of life, and with it, the potential of living eternally. The Bible does not indicate whether they had yet eaten from this tree, but it is quite possible that they had, and that the "effect" of the fruit was limited by time, (i.e., one had to eat regularly to maintain an exemption from death.) Whatever the case, it is certain that prior to the fall, Adam and Eve were not growing closer to death on a daily basis, for death was not something that was expected to happen of itself. When introduced as a judgment, or penalty, death would be a totally new aspect of their lives ... a dreadful consequence of their recently acquired sin.

Now, we have seen in Genesis 2:17 that God gave Adam a specific warning in regard to this penalty for disobedience; death was to be expected "in the day that thou eatest," and God was no doubt feared as being true to His word. But when Adam and Eve did indeed eat, God enacted His punishment not by the execution of His creatures, but by banishing them from the garden immediately lest they "take of the tree of life and eat and live forever." And so, deprived of the fruit from the tree, Adam and Eve began to die from that day on. Every day they advanced closer to death with the onset of the aging process, while simultaneously experiencing the thorns and thistles of life outside Eden.

If we pause to analyze the garden events in more detail at this point, two factors emerge which are of great significance, and these are the principles of mercy and forgiveness. When God confronted Adam and Eve with their sin, He *could* have slain them immediately on the spot, and His words in Genesis 2:17 seem to indicate that he would do so. (Many people, in searching for an answer as to why He did not slay them, have come to believe that an invisible "spiritual death" must have occurred instead ... for God must be true to His word.) But our God is truly a merciful God (Exodus 34:6-7), and Adam and Eve became the first human recipients of His wonderful compassion. Rather than ending their lives at the time of judgment, (or placing them squarely on the road to hell), He banished Adam and Eve from the garden and thus withheld the fruit of the tree of life. They would still indeed die – for the warning of death in Genesis 2:17 was no idle threat – but because of God's mercy the day of their death was delayed.

This mercy may have been granted primarily because Adam and Eve's sin was a result of Satan's deception, and not initially their own idea. The fact that Satan was the first to be condemned (Genesis 3:14-15) may support this view, but it is also very evident that God had a plan for fallen Adam that included many of his descendants. Were it not for God's great mercy, which resulted in a delayed death for Adam and Eve rather than an immediate one, none of us would be here today to experience the grace He gave us all through Jesus Christ our Lord.

The second important factor here is the forgiveness of our God, and this would naturally include His provision for covering His creature's transgressions. As soon as the first man and woman sinned, "the eyes of them both were opened, and they knew that they were naked." They knew good and evil now, and they were all too aware that they had done the wrong thing. Their immediate inclination was to find a covering which would "hide" what seemed to be the glaring evidence of their sin. Although Adam and Eve made themselves aprons to conceal what they now considered to be their shame, the man-made covering was obviously not sufficient. God provided them with a better covering of skins - garments that could have been fashioned only through the blood-shedding sacrifice of animal life.

We can discover here in Genesis, then, the first atonement for sin ... and if we look a little closer, forgiveness through the shedding of blood. Thus God hid man's weakness and covered his shame in a way that was acceptable to Himself: innocent life was given in order to make expiation for the guilty. Soon after would come Abel's respected offering (Genesis 4:4), the bullocks and goats of the Law, and later still, Jesus Christ Himself. It would seem that God had a gracious provision for man's sin just as early as the moment it began. His solution was mercy, forgiveness, and a means of nullifying the sin that had thoroughly tainted His dearly loved creatures.

It is most interesting to note that once man had fallen in Eden, God would not allow him to live "forever" in his sinful state. He banished Adam and Eve from the garden immediately to keep them from partaking of the tree of life and thus becoming immortal sinners. This gives us good reason to question whether God actually intends for any person in the state of sin to exist for eternity, for He obviously moved to prevent such a happening as soon as man's purity became destroyed. In view of God's actions in the garden and His plan to remove sin from His people, it would seem that His intent is to eliminate sin ... not to forever immortalize it.

Knowing all this, we should ask again: Why does man die? Because he must not live forever in his fallen condition! This is the horrible thought left unexpressed in Genesis 3:22 and signified by a dash at the end of the verse. An eternal sinner would be a calamity, for it would allow sin to perpetuate for all time to come. Should such a condition become a reality, God could never make an end of sin, and could never fully cleanse His creation of its filthy corruption. For this reason God promptly cut off the immortality that was originally offered or imparted to Adam and Eve; when sin invaded mankind, the penalty became death in order that sin would assuredly be stopped.

From that day on, man would be looking to God for an answer to sin and death, with the hope of being reinstated to his former standing. Happily, the solution came in the form of Jesus Christ, Who was crucified as an offering for our sin, and resurrected from the dead with the promise that He was the first of many to come. When the Lord returns to Earth a second time, immortality will be granted to His people and He will thereby restore to man what he lost that day in the garden: the saints will be raised in sinless purity, and with the capacity to live forever. At this time the tree of life will also be returned to man, standing unguarded in the new paradise and once again yielding its fruit (Revelation 22:1-2).

3. The Penalty of sin is death!

In addition to the historical testimony of Genesis, the Bible also gives us solid doctrine that confirms the facts of the garden events. In his New Testament epistle to the Romans, the Apostle Paul makes it clear to us that death came into the world through sin, and that death is now a result of sin. He never suggests that the death he speaks of is a "spiritual death," but only teaches of simple death with no additional defining words. We can safely deduce, then, that the death that Paul speaks of is the self-same one spoken of by the Old Testament men of God. Because of the fall of Adam, all men must one day enter "the land of forgetfulness" where they "know not anything" and their bodies turn to dust (Psalm 88:12, Ecclesiastes 9:5).

> By one man sin entered into the world, and death by sin; and so death passed upon all men, for that all have sinned. (Romans 5:12)

Having initially entered the creation through that one first man, sin and death became inherited factors for all who would subsequently be born. Examine the verse closely and you will notice that the teaching of Genesis is reaffirmed here: Adam and Eve had no expectation of death until judgment was pronounced on them, for death entered the creation "by sin," and was therefore not present until sin occurred.[1] In the next

---

[1] Paul's instruction in Romans 5:12 would seem to lend support to the idea that the fruit of the tree of life must be eaten continuously in order to maintain deathlessness, and that it was a forced withdrawal from the fruit which allowed death to begin its work in Adam and Eve. For if these first people did not originally possess some kind of immunity from death, (presumably via the tree), how could death have entered in as a *new* phenomenon "by sin"? If death was not present originally, then some kind of immortality must have been governing Adam and Eve's lives before their fall. Logically, death cannot "enter in" if it is already expected as the natural course of things; thus Adam and Eve would seem to have possessed an exemption from death up until the time that sin occurred, and it's most obvious source was the tree of life which was with them in the garden. (In the same vein, it has also been speculated that Adam and his descendants lived their very extended life spans due to a progressive "wearing off" of the effects of the fruit from the life tree, i.e., following Adam's forced withdrawal.) Again, the Bible does not specifically say if Adam and Even ever ate of the tree of life...it only details what happened when they ate of the forbidden tree. Other views of the garden events may differ from the

passage, we have the unavoidable inheritance from Adam contrasted with the gracious gift granted through the Lord Jesus Christ. Here, as in our first example, we are made aware that it is not only sin that man has received through Adam, but also death, which reigns over us all.

> For if by one man's offence death reigned by one; much more they which receive abundance of grace and of the gift of righteousness shall reign in life by One, Jesus Christ. Therefore as by the offence of one judgment came upon all men to condemnation; even so by the righteousness of One the free gift came upon all men unto justification of life. For as by one man's disobedience many were made sinners, so by the obedience of One shall many be made righteous. (Romans 5:17-19)

Whereas through Adam we were all condemned to sin and death, through Jesus Christ we can obtain the free gift of righteousness which justifies our receiving eternal life. (Those who do not obtain righteousness remain in their sin, and they are therefore not worthy of living forever.) Thus we find that by the actions of Adam man lost his immortality, but by the grace of God he may regain it again through Christ.

> For the wages of sin is death; but the gift of God is eternal life through Jesus Christ our Lord. (Romans 6:23)

Since all men have sinned (Romans 3:23), all men must receive their wages of death, including the people of God. All must die and suffer utter destruction because of the sin which has infected their minds and their bodies - a principle that Paul has referred to as "the law of sin and death" (Romans 8:2). But the gift of eternal life is joyously proclaimed as the solution here: though men will die because of their Adamic sin, they may live again everlastingly because of the gift of Christ. Please note that in the contrast given, the "life" that Paul speaks of is described by the adjective "eternal," whereas the "death" is plain and simple: so that we have "eternal life" vs "death." This particular contrast is often repeated in the New Testament, a situation which seems to imply that there is something very emphatic about the "life," but nothing

---

"fruit theory" mentioned here, but all must bend to Paul's statement that death came into the world by sin.

particularly remarkable about the "death."[2] In our next passage, from 1 Corinthians, Paul reiterates that death came upon man through Adam, but he also teaches that new life will come through Christ by means of the resurrection of the dead.

> Now is Christ risen from the dead, and become the firstfruits of them that slept. For since by man came death, by man came also the resurrection of the dead. For as in Adam all die, even so in Christ shall all be made alive. (1 Corinthians 15:20-22)

The remedy to the problem of sin and death is to be made eternally alive again via the miracle of resurrection. Man cannot escape the fact that he must die because of sin, but he *can* escape the grave through the power of Jesus Christ. And note the contrast: "in Adam all die ... in Christ *shall* all be made alive." This implies that the saints who have "slept" are dead, and are therefore not alive right now beyond the grave; in order to be "made alive" in the future, one must at some point be truly dead. Indeed, sin must do its work in every man, following its course to that certain end:

> When lust hath conceived, it bringeth forth sin; and sin, when it is finished, bringeth forth death. (James 1:15)

James has given us a simple comparison by which he demonstrates that the former in each case causes the latter. So we see that when sin "is finished" in a man, it brings forth his death. And when death finally arrives, the battle with sin is over. Paul states this plainly as a fundamental truth:

> He that is dead is freed from sin." (Romans 6:7)

Sin is the cause of death, but its dominion over a person ceases when that person dies. This is quite logical, for when a man undergoes the

---

[2] Although the term "spiritual death" does not occur in the Scriptures, many people are led by tradition to interpret Romans 6:23 with that concept in mind, adding even the idea of eternal conscious torment where the apostle makes no mention of it all. The reader must make his own decision as to whether or not it is appropriate to interpret in this manner. It is unfortunate that the exact words of Paul are seldom considered as "the truth" today, and there may be but one reason for this: taken literally and simply as written, they do not agree with the prevailing beliefs concerning the immortality of the soul and spirit.

return to dust, there is no longer a medium in which sin can reign. In this way sin is not able to perpetuate, but is instead destroyed in death with the flesh in which it dwelled. Once a man is dead, the wages of sin have been paid to him and his encounter with this enemy is over.

But while death frees a man from sin, it does not follow that he is subsequently worthy of resurrection to eternal life. A man must be *justified* to live forever, and he must seek out this justification while he yet lives. He must find and lay hold on God's accepted sacrifice for sin so that his transgressions will always be covered. Thankfully, there is a way by which sin can be forgiven, a man can be made righteous, and the dominion of death can be overcome. Through Jesus Christ, and through Jesus Christ only, a man can defeat the penalty of sin and one day live forever.

4. Jesus Christ is the solution to sin and death

When man fell into the snare of sin and death, God already had a marvellous plan to redeem His creation and one day restore their lives. We have previously seen that all men have inherited death due to the sinful nature that has been passed down to them through Adam. The following passages will elaborate upon a more happy truth - that God has graciously provided Jesus Christ as the means through which man may inherit eternal life.

> For God so loved the world, that He gave His only begotten Son, that whosoever believeth in Him should not perish, but have everlasting life. (John 3:16)

Jesus Christ is the channel through which eternal life is made available to the world. Eternal life describes an existence that is everlasting, perpetual, and infinite in duration. At no point in Scripture is it ever explained to be life in communion with God as opposed to life in a separate eternal hell. When man is offered "eternal life" or "everlasting life," he is literally being offered perpetual existence ... but by the grace of the Father, and again, only through Jesus Christ:

> "Verily, verily, I say unto you, Moses gave you not that bread from heaven; but My Father giveth you the true bread from heaven. For the bread of God is He Which cometh down from heaven, and giveth life unto the world." (John 6:32-33)

Our Lord gives "life" unto the world, and it is apparent that He is speaking of eternal life. If men were born eternal in nature, Christ could not truly give them such life, for they would already be in possession of it.

> "I am come that they might have life, and that they might have it more abundantly." (John 10:10)

Jesus Christ came into the world so that men *might have* the opportunity of eternal existence. He is truly "the way, the truth, and the life" (John 14:6), and by Him a man may receive the precious gift.

> Where sin abounded, grace did much more abound; that as sin has reigned unto death, even so might grace reign through righteousness unto eternal life by Jesus Christ our Lord. (Romans 5:20-21)

Christ has awarded His people righteousness, that by grace they might receive eternal life through His person. Righteousness enables men to stand before God with their sin not imputed to them; and, with the barrier of sin removed, and the righteousness of Christ standing in its stead, they are then justified and worthy to receive eternal life. Please note that in the passage above, "eternal life" is contrasted with the simple death that is inherited through Adam ... not with a "spiritual death" of the soul or the spirit. The Scriptural opposite of eternal life is death.

> For the wages of sin is death; but the gift of God is eternal life through Jesus Christ our Lord. (Romans 6:23)

This verse - certainly worth repeating - has Paul summing up the doctrine of death-through-Adam and life-through-Christ. The verse contains both a statement of the malady and the wonderful God-given remedy. Jesus Christ solved the problem of sin by offering Himself as the bloody sacrifice that would "cover" men's transgressions. He simultaneously solved the problem of death by dying as man's substitute, and thus receiving the wages of sin for him. Then, as a proof that death might not have permanent dominion over mankind, He was made alive again in a glorious body fitted for eternity. By the wonderful grace of God, Jesus Christ has essentially done away with death, providing man with a way of salvation from that great penalty of sin.

> God ... Who hath saved us, and called us with an holy calling, not according to our works, but according to His own purpose and grace, which was given us in Christ Jesus before the world began, but is now made manifest by the appearing of our Saviour Jesus Christ, Who hath abolished death, and hath brought life and immortality to light through the gospel. (2 Timothy 1:9-10)

God's provision to save us from sin and death was already in place "before the world began"; it was made manifest, or fully realized, when Jesus Christ appeared on the Earth to perform the work of salvation. This He did by taking the form of a human being:

> Forasmuch then as the children are partakers of flesh and blood, He also Himself likewise took part of the same; that through death He might destroy him that had the power of death, that is, the devil; and deliver them who through fear of death were all their lifetime subject to bondage. (Hebrews 2:14-15)

When Jesus Christ took the form of flesh and blood in order to perform the act of atonement, His death not only covered man's sin, but also signalled the inevitable end of Satan. With both sin and its instigator defeated by the cross, the people of God no longer need to fear death as an everlasting consequence of their transgressions. The work of Christ has insured that God will reverse their deaths and restore their lives forever through resurrection. Amazingly and wonderfully, the solution to sin and death came through One Who was simultaneously both a kinsman to man, and the Son of God - a Redeemer Who would invite men to partake of eternal life via the simple act of faith alone.

5. Faith is the key to eternal life

Eternal life is being offered to all of humanity, but it is sadly true that not all men will receive it. It appears that only those who love and seek the righteousness of God through faith will actually make use of His solution to sin and death. Surely this is part of God's grand design, for it would bring into eternity only those who desire to be free from sin and to dwell in peace with the Lord. Those who do not admire God and His ways would be quite "out of place" in the world to come, so in this matter God has given us a choice: we can either choose life with Him, or we can decline His invitation and thereby choose permanent death and destruction.

The passages in this chapter will demonstrate that faith is the specific act which brings eternal life within a man's grasp. The concept of receiving immortality in return for faith is sometimes referred to as "conditional immortality," for God's granting of life is seen to be conditional on whether one has placed his trust in His promises. Please take careful note of the issue being set forth within the verses that follow; often the contrast given is between eternal life and no life at all.

> And as Moses lifted up the serpent in the wilderness, even so must the Son of Man be lifted up; that whosoever believeth in Him should not perish, but have eternal life. For God so loved the world that He gave His only begotten Son, that whosoever believeth in Him should not perish, but have everlasting life. (John 3:14-16)

Faith, or belief, is here established as the key to immortality. Whosoever believes in Jesus Christ shall have eternal/everlasting life, while those who do not believe in Him will perish. The primary meaning of the word "perish" is to become destroyed or to die, and a detailed examination of its Biblical use will follow later in this study. If we refrain from applying the traditional interpretation of "hell" to these verses, we can see by the simple wording that death is the meaning implied:

> He that believeth on the Son hath everlasting life: and he that believeth not the Son shall not see life; but the wrath of God abideth on him. (John 3:36)

Note again the same basic contrast: the faithful are said to have everlasting life, but the unbelieving "shall not see life." If a person is not expected to "see life," the only logical alternative is that once dead, he will remain in the state of death. Thus the wrath of God toward him is expressed not by an eternity of torment, but by the Divine judgment that he is not worthy of resurrection to life. Only by faith can a man one day "see" eternal life, and this life comes only through the name of Jesus Christ:

> But these are written, that ye might believe that Jesus is the Christ, the Son of God; and that believing ye might have life through His name. (John 20:31)

God's simple requirement for eternal life is that we believe in what He has said: that Jesus is the Son of God Who was sent to give life unto the world. It is interesting to note that the great failing of Adam and Eve was that they gave up faith in what God had told them (concerning the tree of knowledge), and instead put their trust in the words of His adversary. They chose to believe what Satan had said, and they did not believe the counsel of their own Creator. Thus when man disobeyed and ate of the forbidden fruit, he fell through a lack of faith in God, and consequently he lost his life. When God offered Christ and His righteousness as the solution to sin and death, faith then became the great litmus test by which man could regain his former standing. If a man will simply believe in Christ, then he is eating of the food which has the power of immortality.

> "Verily, verily, I say unto you, He that believeth on Me hath everlasting life. I am that bread of life. Your fathers did eat manna in the wilderness, and are dead. This is the bread which cometh down from heaven, that a man may eat thereof, and not die. I am the living bread which came down from heaven: if any man eat of this bread, he shall live for ever: and the bread that I will give is My flesh, which I will give for the life of the world." (John 6:47-51)

Here we see that a man who partakes of the living bread (Jesus Christ) "shall live forever." Note that these are the very words that the Lord Himself uses to define everlasting life. Modern preachers often say that the unbelieving also shall live forever, but Jesus Christ taught that such a future is only in store for the faithful: for those who "believeth" in Him. "(Note also, that in speaking to His audience, Christ contrasts everlasting life with the plain death that came upon their "fathers.")

"Except ye eat the flesh of the Son of man, and drink His blood, ye have no life in you" (John 6:53).

It is also interesting to see that the Lord promised His audience that if they believed, they would "not die." This very literal offer was made by Christ when He walked the Earth and proclaimed that the kingdom was "at hand". But it was conditional on whether Israel, as a nation, accepted Him as the Messiah. Had they done so, this present age would have come to an end, and the nation would have entered into kingdom blessings of eternal life at that very time. The faithful who were still living would have been - transformed changed into an incorruptible condition without first experiencing death and resurrection.

But as prophesied, Israel not only did not accept Jesus Christ, they also slew Him. Nevertheless, the nation was given a second chance, and the kingdom offer was continued by the apostles after Christ's ascension. With the kingdom still "at hand," the Apostle Paul taught that those who were alive at the imminent second coming would not die, but would be "changed" from a mortal condition into an immortal one (1 Corinthians 15:50-53). This re-offering of the kingdom, with all of its accompanying signs and wonders, is recorded in the book of Acts and came to a conclusion at Acts 28:28. It was at this point in time that the Lord closed the door on unbelieving Israel, and for a season, opened another door to the Gentiles. The kingdom and the second coming became postponed, and so also was the possibility of avoiding death. We can see the promise of transformation repeated in the latter half of the passage below; here the Lord is promising resurrection for those who have died in the faith, and transformation for the godly who remain alive at the coming of the kingdom.

> "I am the resurrection, and the life: he that believeth in Me, though he were dead, yet shall he live: and whosoever liveth and believeth in Me shall never die." (John 11:25-26)

In these verses Jesus Christ has declared Himself to be the path to both resurrection and eternal life. His promise is given to him "that believeth in Me," with death emerging as the apparent alternative.

> And this is the record, that God hath given to us eternal life, and this life is in His Son. He that hath the Son hath life; and he that hath not the Son of God hath not life. (1 John 5:11-12)

It is easy to conclude that if a man does not "have" Jesus Christ through faith, then he also does not have the expectation of eternal existence. As the Lord has said in John 6:51, only those who eat of the living bread shall "live for ever." Those who do not partake of this life-giving sustenance shall simply not live at all, for the wages of sin is death and the equation is a fundamental one:

$$\text{No Christ} + \text{No Covering For Sin} = \text{No Life.}$$

(If we were to apply the traditional interpretation to the above 1 John passage, and suggest that the faithless will suffer eternal conscious torment, we may rightfully wish to question the resulting contradiction that having "no life" means having a perpetual life in hellfire.)

Now when we see that a man must "have" the Son in order to have eternal life, it is natural for us to wonder how the saints of the Old Testament can be saved when they never even knew the man Jesus. The answer is given to us in chapter four of Romans, where the Apostle Paul writes at length on faith and righteousness. Here we learn that the Old Testament saints obtained righteousness by faithfulness to all that God had revealed to them *in their time*; their faith was "imputed" to them for righteousness; "credited them as righteousness" is how the *New International Version (NIV)* puts it. This righteousness brought them justification of life through the Saviour. For "they which receive abundance of grace and of the gift of righteousness shall reign in life by One, Jesus Christ" (Romans 5:17).

Before departing from the theme of faith and its relationship to eternal existence, there is one more perspective from which we should view the gift of life. While we know that eternal life is "the promise He hath promised us" (1 John 2:25), and that we shall not actually "see" this incorruptible life until resurrection, we will note that it is often spoken of as if it were already possessed:

> Verily, verily, I say unto you, He that heareth My word, and believeth on Him That sent Me, hath everlasting life, and shall not come into condemnation; but is passed from death to life. (John 5:24)

Here the Lord proclaims that His believers have passed from death to life, whereas those who do not believe will come into condemnation. The word rendered "condemnation" here is the Greek *krisis,* which means "judgment." Thus the Lord is warning that the unfaithful will come under the judgment of death, while the godly have already "passed" from this dreaded state. Although the faithful of God are said to "have life" right now, it is apparent from other passages that this is a "promise of life" (2 Timothy 1:1). Indeed, a quick glance at John 3:36 will reveal that "having life" is a reference to the future event of "seeing life" in resurrection. Nevertheless, God's promise of eternal life is so assured that we are said to possess this life even now.

In the same vein, the Bible also teaches the related concept that we are "dead," or lifeless, before the time when we are saved by our act of faith. This is because the unbelieving have the certainty of death residing in them, just as the redeemed are already counted as "having life" (1 John 5:12). Thus, belief and unbelief each have their own distinct and predictable consequences. Those who have no saving faith are said to "abide in death" (1 John 3:14). But when we come to believe in Christ, we are said to be "quickened" (Ephesians 2:5), and to "have passed from death unto life" (1 John 3:14). So whereas before salvation we were as good as dead, after salvation we are as good as alive for eternity. In the next few chapters we will look at death and resurrection more closely in an effort to better understand the path that lies ahead for the faithful.

6. Death is likened to sleep

We have seen that man must die because of sin, and that his death is a state of non-awareness. The Bible often refers to man's death as "sleep," giving us a pleasant and poetic word for what is actually a rather unpleasant concept. The choice of "sleep" in place of death would seem purposed to convey to us the sleep-like characteristics of helpless unconsciousness. "Sleep" would be an odd choice indeed, if God actually intended us to understand death as a wakeful and alert state of mind.

> And the Lord said unto Moses, "Behold, thou shalt sleep with thy fathers." (Deuteronomy 31:16)

The first occurrence of this beautifully conceived euphemism is mostly by implication; the Hebrew speaks of "lying down," (*Shakab*), as lying down to sleep. (The literal meaning behind the word is made clear by verse 14 just before it, in which the Lord says, "thy days approach, that thou must die.") Note the lovely and expressive nature of the next example, in which David prays to be delivered from death.

> Consider and hear me, O Lord my God: lighten mine eyes, lest I sleep the sleep of death. (Psalm 13:3)

It is apparent that this term for death became well known among the earlier peoples; when David finally did "sleep the sleep of death," it was duly noted within the first book of Kings:

> So David slept with his fathers, and was buried in the city of David. (1 Kings 2:10)

Job also uses the concept of lying down to "sleep" when speaking of the state of the dead:

> So man lieth down, and riseth not: till the heavens be no more, they shall not awake, nor be raised out of their sleep. (Job 14:12)

Again we see that the dead are "sleeping," but we also find here that there is a time for "awakening." Many people believe that when "sleep" is used in the Scriptures, it is meant to convey a conscious state of "rest." This, however, does not fully harmonize with the analogy given to us by God, for a man cannot "awake" from a conscious state of rest. One must be truly asleep in order to awake, just as one must be fully dead in order to be "made alive" (1 Corinthians 15:21-22) again through resurrection. The deliberate contrast of "sleeping" with "awakening" shows us that true "sleep" is the proper metaphor to be used when describing the state of death.

We continue to find death as "sleep" in the New Testament, where the story of the raising of Lazarus is of particular interest. Here the Lord carries on the terminology that went before, explaining it to His disciples so that none could fail to understand:

> "Our friend Lazarus sleepeth; but I go, that I may awake him out of sleep." Then said His disciples, "Lord, if he sleep, he shall do well." (Howbeit Jesus spake of his death: but they thought that He had spoken of taking rest in sleep.) Then said Jesus unto them plainly, "Lazarus is dead." (John 11:11-14)

It is quite clear from the words of our Lord that death is likened to sleep, and that resurrection is the corresponding awakening. The wording implies that it was not merely the body of Lazarus that had died, but Lazarus the person: "*Lazarus* is dead." Thus, when resurrection was performed, "he that was dead came forth" from the tomb (John 11:44) ... not he whose body had died.

When we look at the Acts and the epistles, the passage of time and events appears to have brought no change to the way that men of God referred to the dead. Those people who died after the ascension of Jesus Christ are also said to be "sleeping," and this suggests that the sacrifice and resurrection of the Lord had no immediate effect on the death state of man. When Steven was stoned to death in Acts 7:59-8:1, it was written that "... he fell asleep. And Saul was consenting unto his death." As we can see yet again in the verse below, people continued to fall into the profound slumber that comes as a result of Adamic sin.

> "He [Jesus Christ] was seen of above five hundred brethren at once, of whom the greater part remain unto this present, but some are fallen asleep." (1 Corinthians 15:6)

"Sleep" is uniformly used of all of the dead, both in the Old and New Testaments, indicating that death still has dominion over all of these people. With the return of Jesus Christ, however, the saints have the sure and certain hope that the resurrection will bring a glorious return to life.

> But I would not have you to be ignorant, brethren, concerning them which are asleep, that ye sorrow not, even as others which have no hope. For if we believe that Jesus died and rose again, even so them also which sleep in Jesus will God bring with Him. (1 Thessalonians 4:13-14)

The context from which this passage is taken concerns the future return of the Lord and the consequent resurrection and transformation of His saints. Here Paul encourages the Thessalonians not to sorrow over their dead in the same way that the unbelieving would sorrow over theirs, i.e., as if the loss were a permanent one; for the Christian can be strengthened in the knowledge of the resurrection to come, having faith that God raised the Lord and will ("even so") raise his brothers also. (Notably, when Paul writes "concerning them which are asleep," there is no mention of comforting each other with thoughts of joyful souls in the presence of the Lord; rather, the future resurrection is the recommended source of "comfort" that Paul gives his readers when we scan to the chapter's conclusion at verse 18, for it is at that time that a reunion will take place.) Note also here that the saints are not spoken of as being asleep *with* the Lord, but *in* the Lord, meaning they died in the hope of His promise. Therefore Paul speaks of those who "sleep in Jesus" and those who are "dead in Christ" (1 Thessalonians 4:16). There is nothing in the apostle's language to promote the interpretation that the "sleepers" are in the company of the Lord; when one is said to be "asleep in Christ" (1 Corinthians 15:18), one is simply identified with Him in death and designated as one of His people.[3] "Sleep" is an excellent metaphor for this "waiting" time in the grave, for it not only implies a true state of unawareness, but it also allows for the "awakening" known as resurrection:

> And many of them that sleep in the dust of the earth shall awake, some to everlasting life, and some to shame and everlasting contempt. (Daniel 12:2)

---

[3] The Romans 6 doctrine of being "dead *with* Christ," (rather than "in" Him), is a doctrine for the living in which they are to reckon themselves to have died with the Savior, and consequently, to have died to sin and its lifestyle. ("For he that is dead is freed from sin," 6:7.) It is essentially different from the concept discussed here, and it is important that one should not be confused with the other.

"Awakening" in resurrection is God's beautiful and poetic match to His "sleeping" in death. The Holy Spirit's use of the term "awakening" would seem intended to teach us that resurrection is an experience resembling that of returning to consciousness after a period of sleep.

Now we can see by the words of Daniel that the dead will sleep in the dust of the earth" until such time that they awake. This establishes a definite "location" wherein the sleep of death actually takes place (as does Job 7:21). Since the awakening of resurrection is an event which will happen some time in the future, we must allow that all of the dead are still sleeping "in the dust" even now. It follows then, of course, that they cannot be sleeping in paradise, heavenly places, or anywhere else; those who have "fallen asleep" must reside within the grave.

Also note from this verse in Daniel that the "awakening" will not bring the same exact experience for each man who is resurrected; the wording implies judgment, and while some shall awake to the simple glory of eternal life, others will experience shame and God's everlasting contempt. A few readers may see "everlasting contempt" as a euphemism for an eternal hell of punishment but the verse itself makes no statement about a future of conscious torment. In regard to the man of faith, however, one thing is clear – for him, the sleep of death is only a very temporary condition to be followed by an endless period of life. For "he that believeth in Me, though he were dead, yet shall he live" (John 11:25).

The "awakening" from death is also spoken of by David, who in this next verse is looking forward to the time when he will meet the Lord:

> As for me, I will behold Thy face in righteousness: I shall be satisfied, when I awake, with Thy likeness. (Psalm 17:15)

David's words here are not intended to suggest that he will wake up possessing the physical or spiritual likeness of the Lord. An alternate translation from the *NIV* reads, "... when I awake, I will be satisfied with seeing Your likeness." David is therefore indicating that he expects to see the face of the Lord when he awakes in resurrection ... not during the time that he is sleeping in death. "For in death there is no remembrance of Thee: in the grave who shall give Thee thanks?" (Psalm 6:5). Not until David awakes from his sleep will he be able to behold the face of his Creator.

In the New Testament, the idea of "awakening" in resurrection is quite frequent, but its appearance is somewhat hidden by our English translations. The Greek verb *egeiro*, which primarily means "to rouse up from sleep or awaken," is used 70 times in reference to resurrection. The secondary meaning of the word is "to cause to stand up," and this is the meaning we usually see assigned to it in translation, (as in "now is Christ *risen* from the dead," 1 Corinthians 15:20). *Egeiro* is almost exclusively translated as "rise," "risen," "raise," etc., but its use to signify an awakening can be seen in the verse from Ephesians below:

> *Awake* thou that sleepest, and arise from the dead, and Christ shall give thee light. (Ephesians 5:14)

The use of this particular word by the Holy Spirit is a very clever means of suggesting resurrection as an awakening, for any reader who has a knowledge of Greek would recognize both the "waking" and "rising" connotations when the word is used in reference to the dead. There are many instances in which it would be quite acceptable to translate *egeiro* as an awakening, for example in the 1 Corinthians verse that has been partially quoted above. See Matthew 10:8, Luke 24:6, John 12:1, 2 Corinthians 1:9, and Ephesians 1:20 for a few more occurrences of *egeiro*.

It is evident that both "sleeping" and "awakening" are important metaphors that contribute much to our understanding of what truly happens in death. When we acknowledge that God has likened death to the unconscious state of sleep, we are better able to appreciate the teaching put forth by the Psalms, Ecclesiastes, Job, etc. - for in death man "knows not anything," just as in sleep he lies without faculties until he awakes. Though hundreds of years may pass between death and resurrection, time will not be recognized by the saints who are asleep in their graves; death will fall upon them in one swift moment, and eternal life will appear to commence within the very next.

7. What is resurrection?

Resurrection is the miraculous means by which God will one day bestow eternal life upon those who have fallen asleep in Christ. As the divine remedy for death, we can look upon resurrection as the total restoration of a man's former self, which would include not only the body, but also the mind which inhabited it. He Who knows the number of hairs on our heads is also capable of remembering and calling back into existence millions of personalities that are long dead. Such an act is indeed awe- inspiring, and can bring new meaning to the concept of resurrection for those who previously saw God as raising only bodies, rather than people.

> Thou, Which hast shewed me great and sore troubles, shalt quicken me again, and shalt bring me up again from the depths of the earth. (Psalm 71:20)

This is the hope of the saints, to be "quickened," or made alive again after death ... for it is at resurrection that everlasting life will begin. Please notice that the psalmist speaks of being in "the earth" at the time of resurrection, not in the heavens or paradise; he obviously regards the body that goes into the ground at death to be his "self," for he calls it "me." The implication is that he, his person, will be retrieved from the dust by God. When the body is brought up, or raised, the resident mind will come with it, and the psalmist will awaken forever to a new and better life.

> Thy dead men shall live, together with my dead body shall they arise. Awake and sing, ye that dwell in dust: for thy dew is as the dew of herbs, and the earth shall cast out the dead. (Isaiah 26:19)

At death man returns to the dust from which he is made, and at resurrection he shall awake and arise from that dust. The graves shall be opened and the people shall come forth out of them.

> 'Behold, O My People, I will open your graves, and cause you to come up out of your graves, and bring you into the land of Israel. And ye shall know that I am the Lord, when I have opened your graves, O My People, and brought you up out of your graves, and shall put My spirit in you, and ye shall live, and I shall place you in your own land; then shall ye know that

I the Lord have spoken it, and performed it,' saith the Lord. (Ezekiel 37:12-14)

Here we see that God will accomplish the restoration of Israel through the raising of the dead. Note the language that He uses in referring to the resurrected ones: "I will open your graves and cause *you* to come up ... and shall put My spirit in you, and ye shall live." Again, the implication is that persons reside in the grave, and that persons shall be resurrected to life. God also says that when He brings the people out of the graves, He will put *His* spirit into that which He has raised - not *their* spirits, or *their* immortal souls. The Lord does not say that He will cause "empty" bodies to come up so that they might be re-inhabited by the eternally living spirits of men. Rather, the sleeping saint "waits" silently in the grave for God to "remember" him ... waits for the "change" that will bring him from death back to life:

> So man lieth down, and riseth not: till the heavens be no more they shall not awake, nor be raised out of their sleep. O that Thou wouldest hide me in the grave, that Thou wouldest keep me secret, until Thy wrath be past, that Thou wouldest appoint me a set time, and remember me! If a man die, shall he live again? all the days of my appointed time will I wait, till my change come. Thou shalt call, and I will answer Thee: Thou wilt have a desire to the work of Thine hands. (Job 14:12-15)

Job knew that he was to spend an "appointed time" in the grave and that this would be followed by the "change" of resurrection. He was so unsettled by what he perceived to be wrathful events from God, that he spoke of "hiding" in death in order to bypass his present sorrows. The entire passage is a truly beautiful one and sets before us a wonderful expectation: "Thou shalt call, and I will answer Thee." At the appointed time we will be awakened out of our "sleep" by the sound of His voice calling; it is sure to be a wondrous moment as we open our new eyes and behold the life promised us through Jesus Christ.

As we move on to the New Testament, we find that resurrection is often spoken of by the Lord Himself ... and not surprisingly, for He has said that He *is* "the resurrection." Even so, the power to resurrect seems to be attributed jointly to the Father and the Son:

> "The Father loveth the Son, and sheweth Him all things that Himself doeth: and He will shew Him greater works than these, that ye may marvel. For as the Father raiseth up the dead, and

quickeneth them; even so the Son quickeneth whom He will. For the Father judgeth no man, but hath committed all judgment unto the Son." (John 5:20-22)

We see again that resurrection is both a raising (a bringing up), and a quickening, or a making alive. In speaking of this marvellous work, Christ uses the word *egeiro* ("raiseth"), and thereby implies that the people will be roused up from the sleep of death. He also reiterates the importance of faith, for the Son is promising everlasting life to all those who trust in Him:

> And this is the Father's will Which hath sent Me, that of all which He hath given Me I should lose nothing, but should raise it up again at the last day. And this is the will of Him That sent Me, that every one which seeth the Son, and believeth on Him, may have everlasting life: and I will raise him up at the last day. (John 6:39-40)

The Son will remember and raise every man that "believeth on Him", granting eternal life "at the last day." As we noted earlier in a quotation from Job (14:15), the Lord will call when the appointed time in the grave is over.

> Verily, verily, I say unto you, The hour is coming, and now is, when the dead shall hear the voice of the Son of God: and they that hear shall live. For as the Father hath life in Himself; so hath He given to the Son to have life in Himself; and hath given Him authority to execute judgment also, because He is the Son of man. Marvel not at this: for the hour is coming, in the which all that are in the graves shall hear His voice, and shall come forth; they that have done good, unto the resurrection of life; and they that have done evil, unto the resurrection of damnation. (John 5:25-29)

Resurrection is a return to life. They that hear the voice shall live, for the Father has life in Himself, and He has given this power of life to Jesus Christ. Please note that the people who will hear the voice of God at resurrection are said to be "in the graves" ... not in the heavens. Those who have been sleeping in the dust shall "come forth" to life and judgment. The Lord also says that the dead – not the bodies of the dead – will live *when they hear the voice*, indicating that immediately before they hear the voice they are not alive. Thus resurrection reverses the state of death in the grave, awakening one from "sleep" and causing him to come forth.

As we saw previously in Daniel 12:2, resurrection will apparently not bring the same experience to all. Here we read of "the resurrection of life" and "the resurrection of damnation," while Daniel spoke of "everlasting life" and "shame and contempt." At this point it is useful to know that the word translated "damnation" here in John is the Greek *Krisis* again, which means "judgment" (as in verses 22 and 27 of this same chapter). The translator's use of the work "damnation" tends to stir up thoughts of an eternal hell, whereas "the resurrection of judgment" simply alerts us that the passing of a sentence is at hand. The *NIV* translation has, "those who have done evil will rise to be condemned," which conveys the thought accurately.

While the resurrection of the saints is to be a total redemption from death and the grave, it is also evident that it will be much more than just that. When man rises up at the appointed time, he is not to reappear in exactly the same state as he was previously; Christ makes this clear while He is answering the Sadducees' question about resurrection.

> "The children of this world marry, and are given in marriage: but they which shall be accounted worthy to obtain that world, and the resurrection from the dead, neither marry or are given in marriage: neither can they die anymore: for they are equal unto the angels; and are the children of God, being the children of the resurrection." (Luke 20:34-36)

The apostle Paul also speaks of there being a difference in the resurrection life to come, explaining to the Corinthians that men will be raised in a new and spiritual form:

> All flesh is not the same flesh: but there is one kind of flesh of men, another flesh of beasts, another of fishes, and another of birds. There are also celestial bodies, and bodies terrestrial: but the glory of the celestial is one, and the glory of the terrestrial is another. There is one glory of the sun, and another glory of the moon, and another glory of the stars: for one star differeth from another star in glory. So also is the resurrection of the dead. It is sown in corruption; it is raised in incorruption: it is sown in dishonour; it is raised in glory: it is sown in weakness; it is raised in power: it is sown a natural body; it is raised a spiritual

body. There is a natural body, and there is a spiritual body. (1 Corinthians 15:39-44)

When the people of God wake up in resurrection he will find that an essential transformation has been made: "The Lord Jesus Christ ... shall change our vile body, that it may be fashioned like unto His glorious body" (Philippians 3:21). Corruption, dishonor and weakness - all manifestations of sin - will be replaced with incorruption, glory and power. A new mind will inhabit this body which will no longer be according to the flesh, and that which is good and right shall be written in the heart. Thus, the people of God shall rise up to meet their Creator as ones who are fully worthy to stand in His company.

> Beloved, now we are the sons of God, and it doth not yet appear what we shall be: but we know that, when He shall appear, we shall be like Him; for we shall see Him as He is. (1 John 3:2)

8. Resurrection will bring us into the presence of the Lord

Many of us have heard from our youth that we will enter into the presence of God at the moment we pass away. Even the term "pass away," (which is human in origin), suggests a "passing" from one world into another, so that death is represented as a doorway through which we exit this life and immediately enter new life with the Lord. This can be acknowledged to be true to a certain extent, for our time spent "sleeping" shall speed by unnoticed and death shall indeed quickly bring us to our new home. But in reality, those who are asleep in Christ are in waiting, silent in the grave and dissolved into dust; they will not come into the presence of Jesus Christ until the appointed time of His own choosing ... when He returns to the Earth and raises them up in glory at the last day.

> Then said Jesus unto them, "Yet a little while I am with you, and then I go unto Him That sent Me. Ye shall seek Me, and shall not find Me: and where I am, thither ye cannot come." (John 7:33-34)

When the Lord ascended to be with the Father, He went to a place where men could not come. (He obviously speaks of the ascension here, and not the period between His death and resurrection, for Matthew 12:40 confirms that the Lord spent "three days and three nights in the heart of the earth" ..... and therefore spent none of that time with "Him That sent Me.") As we have previously seen in 1 Timothy 6:16, Jesus Christ is now "dwelling in the light which no man can approach unto." Alive or dead, we cannot see Him, cannot be with Him. We must look instead for the season in which the separation will be remedied.

> Simon Peter said unto Him, "Lord, whither goest Thou?" Jesus answered him, "Whither I go, thou canst not follow Me now; but thou shalt follow Me afterwards ... In My Father's house are many mansions: if it were not so, I would have told you. I go to prepare a place for you. And if I go and prepare a place for you, I will come again, and receive you unto Myself; that where I am, there ye may be also." (John 13:36, 14:2-3)

Here the Lord establishes His second coming as the moment when He shall be reunited with mankind. Only after He returns to "receive" us can we be with Him...and only then can we enter the place that He is preparing for us now. It is not unusual for us to hear people say that Jesus Christ has been receiving the faithful dead unto Himself since He ascended into the heavens; and we often hear it said that He "calls them home" when their life is ended. But we can see by His words here that His return is the great moment we should hope for; since man cannot go where the Lord is, he must simply wait until the Lord returns to him.

> "Let not your heart be troubled, neither let it be afraid. Ye have heard how I said unto you, I go away, and come again unto you." (John 14:27-28)

The parting hope that Jesus Christ left to His disciples was the hope that *He* would come again unto *them* ... not the hope that they might come unto Him upon their deaths. When He returns to the earth, all those who have been waiting for the Lord shall meet Him. The dead who have waited in the grave shall be quickened, and the living shall be "changed," so that both groups may witness His triumphant revelation as the Son of God.

> For as in Adam all die, even so in Christ shall all be made alive. But every man in his own order: Christ the firstfruits; afterward they that are Christ's, *at His coming*. (1 Corinthians 15:22-23)

> Behold I show you a mystery; We shall not all sleep, but we shall all be changed, in a moment, in the twinkling of an eye, *at the last trump*: for the trumpet shall sound, and the dead shall be raised incorruptible, and we shall be changed. (1 Corinthians 15:51-52)

While resurrection is the hope for the majority of God's people, those who are alive at the return of Christ shall instead experience the miracle of transformation. These shall not die, or "sleep," but shall be "changed" from their natural bodies to their new spiritual bodies at the last trump (the seventh trumpet of Revelation 11:15). Thus, in the latter of the above passages, Paul speaks of two separate events which will occur at the second coming: 1) the dead shall be raised, and 2) "we" (the living) shall be changed into an incorruptible state. (Paul himself speaks as though he expected to be alive at the Lord's return, for the time which Israel was being offered the kingdom had not yet expired, and the kingdom, therefore, had not yet been postponed.) In the passage below, Paul gives a more detailed account of how both the dead and the living will enter into the presence of the Lord. Note his insistent statement that those who are alive at the coming shall not "prevent," or act ahead of, the dead.

> For this we say unto you by the word of the Lord, that we which are alive and remain unto the coming of the Lord, shall not prevent them which are asleep. For the Lord Himself shall descend from heaven with a shout, with the voice of the archangel, and with the trump of God: and the dead in Christ shall rise first: then we which are alive, and remain, shall be caught up together with them in the clouds, to meet the Lord in the air: and so shall we ever be with the Lord. (1 Thessalonians 4:15-17)

The order of the events is clear: the Lord shall descend, the dead shall rise, and then the living will "be caught up together with them" so that both will meet the Lord simultaneously in the air. In this way, either by resurrection or transformation, the saints shall be with the Lord for ever. Those who "love His appearing" (2 Timothy 4:8) shall be made alive for eternity when Christ, Who is our life, shines forth:

> For ye are dead, and your life is hid with Christ in God. When Christ, Who is our life, shall appear, then shall ye also appear with Him in glory. (Colossians 3:3-4)

When the Saviour appears, then we will appear with Him. This does not mean that our persons will have previously been in His company as disembodied souls or spirits. It means that we will appear with Christ by way of resurrection or the "change" of transformation. Note that in this passage, Paul is in the midst of addressing a doctrine we touched on earlier - that of the living reckoning themselves as "dead with Christ." Even though the death spoken of here is a reckoned one, it may one day become a reality for us, and is already a reality for many others. Of particular interest is the apostle's statement to the effect that while we are dead, our "life is hid with Christ in God." Although we will no longer have any being in the death state, in a sense we will continue to exist in the mind of God, where our lives have been laid up in store for us. When Christ, Who is our life, appears, then our lives shall be brought forth from their hiding place. We shall appear with Him in glorious refashioned bodies, for this will be the wonderful moment when the gift of life is ours in every sense.

> For I know that my Redeemer liveth, and that He shall stand at the latter day upon the earth: and though after my skin worms

destroy this body, yet in my flesh shall I see God. (Job 19:25-26)

Now the Scriptures have shown us that the hope of the faithful man is to be made alive at the Lord's return, but we can also see by the book of Revelation that not all men are to be raised at once. There are two separate resurrections revealed through John's vision, and those not counted worthy of the first resurrection are said to remain dead for an additional 1000 years. Many readers give little attention to the fact that the Scriptures have spoken of a "better" resurrection; that is, an earlier resurrection that is a reward for the faithful who overcome tribulation or are martyred for the sake of the Lamb and the word of God. Hebrews 11:35 speaks of Old Testament people who sought this resurrection with their great faith, and many others shall earn it during the end-time trouble to come. Those who are chosen will be people of superior standing whose acts have merited them the honor of wearing a crown of life and reigning with Christ throughout the millennium to come. By virtue of their deeds they are evidently not the entire of redeemed mankind, but a very elite group.

> And I saw thrones, and they sat upon them, and judgment was given unto them; and I saw the souls of them that were beheaded for the witness of Jesus, and for the word of God, and which had not worshipped the beast, neither his image, neither had received his mark upon their foreheads, or in their hands; and they lived and reigned with Christ a thousand years. But the rest of the dead lived not again until the thousand years were finished. This is the first resurrection. (Revelation 20:4-5)

While the people mentioned here are obviously champions of the faith, we should not disallow that others with somewhat lesser achievements may also be raised at this time. (Since the subject of Revelation is the great tribulation, it would not seem illogical for this particular book to stress the rewards to be expected by those who overcome the trials of that period.) But, a resurrection "at His coming" has been promised for those "that are Christ's" (1 Corinthians 15:23), and we have also just seen it said that those who have been identified with Him, and died with Him (Romans 6:3-11), shall "appear with Him" when He appears. Even so, it is apparent that the first resurrection is a selection of the worthy, with some people being left behind in the grave until a later time.

Note also that the language used in the above passage strongly suggests that the dead are truly dead until they live again via resurrection – for John writes that the rest of the dead "lived not again" until the 1000 years were finished. By this he indicates that there is an additional group of people who yet remain in death, and who are therefore not alive. These continue to sleep in the dust until they, too, are raised to life and judgment.

> And I saw a great white throne, and Him That sat on it, from Whose face the earth and the heaven fled away; and there was found no place for them. And I saw the dead, small and great, stand before God; and the books were opened: and another book was opened, which is the book of life: and the dead were judged out of those things which were written in the books, according to their works. And the sea gave up the dead which were in it; and death and hell delivered up the dead which were in them: and they were judged every man according to their works. And death and hell were cast into the lake of fire. This is the second death. And whosoever was not found written in the book of life was cast into the lake of fire. (Revelation 20:11-15)

Whereas the first resurrection will raise Christ's highly honoured faithful, the second resurrection will bring forth a greater mass of people, some percentage of which will enter into the lake of fire. The presence of the lake suggests that this round of judgment will be considerably harsher than the first, and the "second death" is suggestive that there is some sort of "end" in sight. It is often taught that the second resurrection will consist only of the unsaved, but it should be noted that the verses here in Revelation 20 never specifically mention the spiritual standing of those who stand before the throne. In addition, we can see by the wording that some of the individuals present will have their names written in the book of life – a title which hardly implies condemnation – for "whosoever was not found written in the book" was cast into the lake. Such words would seem to indicate that some names *were* found, for if no names were discovered at all, we would expect to read that everyone was put into the lake. It seems evident, then, that the second resurrection is not simply a resurrection and condemnation of the unredeemed. Various interpretations of the Scriptures have led to a number of different views as to precisely what groups of people might be raised at this time.

In brief summary, Jesus Christ is now ascended to the Father and "dwelling in the light which no man can approach unto." Although we cannot presently follow Him or be with Him, He has promised the faithful that He will "come again." at which time His sleeping shall awake and His living shall be "come again,." at which time His sleeping shall awake and His living shall be "changed," or transformed. For the millions of faithful who lie asleep, the awakening of resurrection will be the moment when they shall behold the likeness of the Lord (Psalm 17:15); therefore it is Christ's second coming or appearing, that holds so much hope for us, for this will be the moment when "we shall see Him as He is" (1 John 3:2).

9. Now is Christ risen from the dead

If we understand resurrection to be the only means of attaining to life after death, then we will also allow that except for Jesus Christ, no person is now alive beyond the grave. While there are several accounts of the raising of the dead in the Bible, all of them differ essentially from the all-important resurrection of Christ. Those men and women who were raised by a prophet, an apostle, or the Lord Himself, were always brought back to life within their natural earthly bodies, and it is universally agreed that they later died natural deaths. Christ, however, was the first to be raised in a glorious incorruptible body ... a spiritual body that was changed and different from the one He walked the Earth in. He did not later die a natural death, but instead ascended into the heavens as One Who is alive for all of eternity. Therefore, Jesus Christ is the first to possess the incorruptible everlasting life that has been promised to the faithful at resurrection. Whereas He was once dead, He is now alive, and to this day He remains the only One who can lay claim to such a state.

What happened to Jesus Christ, then, was a demonstration of our own future hope, and the proof positive that God could indeed work His promise of raising the dead incorruptible. Because of His unique status, one of the many titles given to the Lord is that of the "Firstborn from the dead":

> And He is the Head of the body, the church: Who is the beginning, the Firstborn from the dead; that in all things He might have the pre-eminence. (Colossians 1:18)

Jesus Christ became the "Firstborn from the dead" so "that in all things He might have the pre-eminence." If any other person experienced life after death before Him, this would rob Him of His position as the first to be reborn into life. Paul's use of the word "firstborn" leads us to perceive resurrection as a kind of birth, or another beginning of life for those who will receive the promise. (Therefore, we are able to view resurrection not as a mere rebodying of already living eternal souls, but as a re-entrance into life from the complete emptiness of the death state.) Jesus Christ has already experienced this rebirth, and so He can say in truth, "I am He that liveth, and was dead; and behold, I am alive for evermore" (Revelation 1:18). Our great hope is to be like Him, to rise again after death has overcome us ... to follow in the footsteps of the "First Begotten of the dead."

> Jesus Christ, Who is the faithful Witness, and the First Begotten of the dead, and the Prince of the kings of the earth. (Revelation 1:5)

Here the Lord is designated as the first offspring of the dead, or the first One brought forth from the grave into life. The word "begotten" again suggests a birth, and Christ can be seen as the first progeny of those under death's dominion. In his initial epistle to the Corinthians, Paul also refers to the Lord as the "firstfruits" of the dead, signifying that He is the earliest gathered fruit from the "crop" to be offered up to God (Leviticus 23:10-14). Though many had died before Him, Jesus Christ was, and still is, the first to be made alive again.

> If in this life only we have hope in Christ, we are of all men most miserable. But now is Christ risen from the dead, and become the firstfruits of them that slept. For since by man came death, by man came also the resurrection of the dead. For as in Adam all die, even so in Christ shall all be made alive. But every man in his own order: Christ the firstfruits; afterward they that are Christs, at His coming. (1 Corinthians 15:19-21)

The wording in this (by now very familiar) passage indicates that the Lord is the only One Who is living beyond the grave; for if the dead in Christ "shall" be made alive at His future second coming, they cannot be alive right now at this moment. Thus, only the "Firstfruits" is alive now, and when He eventually appears to us in glory and is revealed as the Son of God, His dead ones will awaken out of their sleep in the dust and join Him forever in eternal life.

It is apparent, then, that the raising of the dead is the great foundation stone of the Christian faith, for without it we would indeed be "most miserable," as Paul says. Without the future hope of resurrection, we would have "this life only" to live, and then an eternity of utter death. But while our own resurrection is essential to our realization of life beyond the grave, even more essential is the raising of Christ. When the Son of God came to the earth He purchased us life itself with His precious blood and He truly gave us one more time to live. While His death on the cross is often regarded as the single great event which has allowed this generous gift, we can see from the writings of Paul that His resurrection was the all important factor in the mechanics of our salvation. Without the resurrection of Jesus Christ, both sin and death maintain their dominion over mankind:

> And if Christ be not raised, your faith is vain; ye are yet in your sins. Then they also which are fallen asleep in Christ are perished. (1 Corinthians 15:17-18)

Our faith is a waste of time and energy if we look to a Saviour who did not rise from the dead. A Saviour who did not defeat death itself has not saved us from that great penalty of sin. Thus, the Apostle Paul makes a startling claim here: if Jesus Christ had not risen from the grave and defied death, then all those who have fallen asleep in Him would be "perished" ... they wouldn't be disembodied souls destined for eternity in hell, but rather they would be forever lost to death with no possibility of retrieval. His own people would never see life again, implying that there is no ongoing existence beyond the grave outside of the eternal life we can inherit through Christ. Indeed, if the Lord did not rise to life, and so, conquer death, then there is no hope that we shall have any life again either. And this is not simply a matter of fact, but it is also a matter of faith. If His resurrection is to be of any benefit to us at all, we must believe that it actually happened:

> If thou shalt confess with thy mouth the Lord Jesus, and shalt believe in thine heart that God hath raised Him from the dead, thou shalt be saved. (Romans 10:9)

When the death of man is acknowledged as a complete loss of being, resurrection is elevated to its proper position: it is the only means by which eternal existence may begin for those who have entered the grave. The raising of the dead comes into perspective as the basis of both the Old Testament hope and the New Testament gospel; for we can see that the people of both time periods looked forward to resurrection as the fundamental solution to the Adamic death that falls upon all men. In modern times, the hope of resurrection is rarely given the preeminent position that it possesses in the books of the Bible. Death is widely proclaimed as the event which will bring the redeemed into the immediate presence of Jesus Christ, and so death has become the hope of many of today's Christians. The end result is that resurrection becomes a much lesser hope...not the blessed hope of eternal life, but the hope of re-embodiment for the "eternal soul."

10. What is the soul?
(*nephesh/psuche*)

At this point in our inquiry about the nature of man, several word studies will be introduced in order to search out the Biblical meanings of the words "soul," "spirit," "hell," and "hell fire." We will also investigate what the Scriptures have to say about the fate of the unredeemed, with special attention to the words "perish," and "destroy."

There is no doubt that we owe a great debt to those who have translated the word of God into our own language, yet at the same time we have to remember that our understanding is contingent upon the accuracy of their translations. The translators of the *KJV* were not always consistent in rendering a Hebrew or Greek word with the same English word each time it occurred. Now it is true that this is not always practical - or desirable - but sometimes the rendering will unquestionably make a difference as to what conclusions we draw.

It is only natural that if a translator is predisposed towards a particular doctrinal view, he may translate with a certain degree of bias as he selects equivalent words. Thus a belief in the "immortal soul" would be likely to color a translation, especially when words are chosen that tend to gently reinforce such a belief. When this indeed happens, we often find that there is measurable information "hidden" behind the translation that we are given. Knowing this, it becomes vitally important for the Bible student to become aware of the Hebrew and Greek words that God employed to teach us about our nature. Awareness of where these words occur, and observance of the context in which they are used, can be a tremendous step towards a better understanding of Biblical truth.

An additional concern of the student is that of establishing accurate definitions for these key doctrinal words. The most reliable way to define a word in question is to let Scripture itself provide a definition. Even a novice can learn a great deal about a word by studying its every occurrence and observing how it is used in sentences - a bit of detective work, but well worth the effort. By doing this we can discover not only what a word does mean, but just as importantly, what it does not mean. (i.e., what the context shows us it cannot mean). The studies provided here are for the most part abridged, serving to demonstrate a method by which the English speaking student may research. Extended study with the aid of Hebrew and Greek concordances is highly recommended.

In the word studies that follow, italics have been used to identify the specific English words in a passage that are the direct translation of the Hebrew or Greek words under discussion. Often the Hebrew or Greek word will be represented by two or more English words, sometimes not occurring adjacent to each other. This is due to the appearance of the Hebrew or Greek word in its various verb forms, and exhibits the translator's attempt to present a grammatically correct English sentence. When the personal pronoun is implied in the verb (rather than expressed by additional words), it too has been put in italics.

As we have noted before, the Bible nowhere speaks of an "immortal soul" or an "eternal soul." (Neither does it mention an "undying soul," "everlasting soul," "deathless soul," or any other similar descriptive term.) The writers of Scripture never specifically described "the soul" in a manner that would lend it immortality, so we should be careful about adding adjectives which might suggest ideas that differ from the original writings. Thus, when searching for information concerning "the soul," it is probably advantageous to start off with just plain "soul" in mind, adding no words or concepts but those that the Bible will show us as we go along.

The word "soul" is an English translation of the Hebrew *nephesh* in the Old Testament and the Greek *psuche* in the New Testament. *Nephesh*, which we shall look at first, occurs 754 times, and although translated 44 (!) different ways in the *KJV*, is mostly rendered "life" or "soul," but sometimes "creature" or "person." The following verses will help to establish a definition for "*nephesh*/soul" by observing the circumstances under which it appears.

> And God said, "Let the waters bring forth abundantly the moving creature that hath life, and fowl that may fly above the earth in the open firmament of heaven." And God created great whales, and every living creature that moveth. (Genesis 1:20-21)

These are the first two occurrences of *nephesh* in the Bible, translated as "life" and as "creature." The first example shows us that God's moving creatures *have* soul; they do not have *a* soul but they *have soul*, which says something different. The second example tells us by its wording that they also *are* souls. Soul, or *nephesh*, is relevant to the fact that they live and move, for soul is life – or secondarily, a living, moving thing that possesses life.

> And God said, "Let the earth bring forth the living creature after his kind, cattle, and creeping thing, and beast of the earth after his kind:" and it was so. (Genesis 1:24)

It is apparent that *nephesh*/soul is used of all of the animals. (See also Genesis 1:30, where God uses this word to speak of "everything that creepeth upon the earth, wherein there is *life*.") Those living things which have soul are distinguished by the fact that they move, or "creep". In Genesis 2, we shall find the first occurrence in which *nephesh* is used of man:

> And the Lord God formed man of the dust of the ground, and breathed into his nostrils the breath of life; and man became a living soul. (Genesis 2:7)

When man received the breath of life from God, he, too, became a soul. Both man and beast are described as *"chay nephesh"* (living soul) at creation, and they are therefore alike in this particular aspect of their being. But notice how the KJV translators chose the English word "creature" for the animals, and "soul" for man, thereby permitting this important similarity to pass unnoticed. As in the case of the animals, it is correct to say of man that he both *has* soul, and that he *is* a soul, for he not only has life, but he also is a life - a living and moving creature. The possession of soul in man and beast is more clearly expressed in the next example, where Job uses *nephesh* in an all inclusive manner.

> Who knoweth not in all these that the hand of the Lord hath wrought this? In Whose hand is *the soul* of every living thing, and the breath of all mankind. (Job 12:9-10)

When "soul" is understood to be "life," there is no difficulty in allowing that both man and beast possess it fully. The Scriptures indicate that both are living, moving, and breathing creatures - both are *"chay nephesh"* - and so it would seem that both have the same soul. Also common to man and beast is the possession of blood, that life-giving fluid to which God attaches very special significance. When Noah and his family were told that the animals would be meat for them, the Lord gave particular instructions as to flesh with the *"nephesh"* remaining in it.

But flesh *with the life thereof*, which is the blood thereof, shall ye not eat. (Genesis 9:4)

God commanded that Noah and his family were not to eat animal flesh with the blood remaining in it. He symbolically equated blood with *nephesh*, because He wished them to understand that blood, like soul, constitutes life itself. Both are givers of life in that both furnish the essential elements that maintain it. This similitude between blood and soul continued to be stressed in the law, where the commandment to refrain from blood is solemnly repeated:

Be sure that thou eat not the blood: for the blood is the life; and thou mayest not eat the life with the flesh. Thou shalt not eat it; thou shalt pour it upon the earth as water. (Deuteronomy 12:23-24)

When the blood of an animal is poured out onto the ground, its soul, or its life, is also figuratively "poured out." Blood represents the life which God has given to His creatures, and because of this symbolic value, it was not to be eaten. The close association of blood with *nephesh* was an important factor in the animal sacrifice of the Law, where animal life was offered as a foreshadowing of the greater sacrifice to come. Even as animal blood was representative of life, so also was our Lord's blood when it was shed at the cross: His loss of blood signified that His life had been given for ours. Without the shedding of His blood, and especially the death that resulted from it, there would have been no remission of sin for mankind (Hebrews 9:22).

In the next example we see *nephesh* used in a somewhat different sense, showing us that human beings who *have soul*, are commonly referred to as souls themselves:

These be the sons of Leah, which she bare unto Jacob in Padanaram, with his daughter Dinah: all *the souls* of his sons and his daughters were thirty and three. (Genesis 46:15)

Souls are creatures with life, so that in this occurrence we should understand them to be "persons." When referring to human beings, sometimes the translators used "souls," and other times they used "persons," as in "threescore and ten *persons*" in Deuteronomy 10:22. *Nephesh* is also frequently used in the sense of a personal pronoun, as is seen in the verse below.

And make me savoury meat, such as I love, and bring it to me, that I may eat; that *my soul* may bless thee before I die. (Genesis 27:4)

"My soul" is the same as "me," "myself," or "I". Here Isaac promises to bless his son Esau before his death, but it is Isaac himself that will give the blessing, not "Isaac's soul." His words are an example of the figure of speech synecdoche (of the part), in which a part of something is put for the whole of it. In this case an essential aspect of man (the soul, or the life) is put for the entire being. Another example of synecdoche can be seen in Romans 3:15, where we read, "Their feet are swift to shed blood." In both cases the ordinary pronouns are enhanced by the figurative use of essential components of the man. (A man has eyes, nose, feet, and a brain – and he also has life/soul.) As in the case of all figures of speech, the object is simply to emphasize.

The English translation of "my soul" is a proper and literal one, but it can sometimes lead readers to the conclusion that the speaker has a soulish entity which performs various actions, or has emotional sensitivity. Attributes which are meant to apply to the person, are then mistakenly attributed to "his soul." When we read "my soul refused" (Psalm 77:2), "my soul hateth" (Isaiah 1:14), or "my soul shall weep" (Jeremiah 13:17), the proper meaning behind the figure of speech is that "I refused," "I hateth," and "I shall weep." The person himself performs all acts and is the source of all feelings. Thus when *nephesh* is used as a personal pronoun in the verse below, we understand it to mean that the psalmist himself has escaped the grip of death.

Unless the Lord had been my help, my soul had almost dwelt in silence. (Psalm 94:17)

Without the help of the Lord, he - not his eternal soul - would have dwelt in the silence of the grave. When the reader is unaware of the use of synecdoche here, the presence of the words "my soul" may seem to support the traditional doctrine of man's inherent immortality; notice how the translators made a switch away from these words when their use might have tended to dispel the traditional view:

Let *me* die the death of the righteous, and let my last end be like his! (Numbers 23:10)

It is very probable that the personal beliefs of the translators led them to avoid the use of "my soul" in this verse. The more consistent rendering

- "Let *my soul* die the death of the righteous" - would undoubtedly suggest that "the soul" of the righteous man is subject to death, and so the less literal "me" was chosen instead. Unfortunately, this action has prevented the English reader from obtaining an accurate understanding of the verse. The use of "me" is not incorrect here, for *nephesh* is being used as a personal pronoun; but "me" has served to hide the fact that *nephesh* is used here, and that the *nephesh*/soul being spoken of is decidedly mortal. The words of Reuben in Genesis 37:21 are likewise rendered, "Let us not kill *him*," when again, a consistent translation would read, "Let us not kill *his soul*." The mortality of *nephesh* continues to be evident when we examine its occurrences in other types of passages:

> And surely your blood of your lives will I require; at the hand of every beast will I require it, and at the hand of man; at the hand of every man's brother will I require the life of man. Whoso sheddeth man's blood, by man shall his blood be shed. (Genesis 9:5-6)

In this example, God tells Noah and his sons that He will require the blood of their souls, indeed their very lives, if they take the life of another person. A soul is a life, and that life can be lost; in some cases it may come to a premature end by the shedding of blood in murder or capital punishment.

> And he that killeth any man shall surely be put to death. And he that killeth a beast shall make it good; beast for beast. (Leviticus 24:17-18)

When a man kills the *nephesh* of another man, he shall be put to death; if he kills the *nephesh* of another man's beast he shall make it good, *nephesh* for *nephesh* ... soul for soul ... life for life.

> If men strive, and hurt a woman with child, so that her fruit depart from her, and yet no mischief follow: he shall be surely punished, according as the woman's husband will lay upon him; and he shall pay as the judges determine. And if any mischief follow, then thou shall give life for life, eye for eye, tooth for tooth, hand for hand, foot for foot, burning for burning, wound for wound, stripe for stripe. (Exodus 21:22-25)

The soul is again seen to be taken by man in capital punishment; even as the hand or the foot is taken, the life is forfeit if a murder has been committed.

> Behold, all *souls* are Mine; *as the soul of* the father, *so also the soul of* the son is Mine: *the soul* that sinneth, it shall die. But if a man be just, and do that which is lawful and right, ... hath walked in My statutes, and hath kept my judgments, to deal truly; he is just, he shall surely live, saith the Lord God. If he beget a son that is a robber, a shedder of blood, and that doeth the like to any one of these things ... shall he then live? he shall not live; he hath done all these abominations; he shall surely die; his blood shall be upon him. (Ezekiel 18:4-5,9-10,13)

In administering her society, Israel was instructed by the Lord to execute those who committed serious breaches of the law. They were to exact the penalty for sin immediately to rid the community of the lawless. Read Leviticus 20 for more on capital punishment and note the repeated use of the phrase "their blood shall be upon them" (verses 9,11,12,13,16,27). The presence of these words in this Ezekiel passage shows us that the death called for here is one in which the *nephesh/* soul would be stoned. The soul that sinned would die a bloody death by the hands of the People ... not a "spiritual death," as is often suggested.

The mortality of the soul can also be seen in the following verse from Genesis, in which Abraham's nephew Lot receives a warning from the Lord. After the angels brought his family out of Sodom, he is told, in today's words, to "run for his life."

> And it came to pass, when they had brought them forth abroad, that He said, "Escape for thy life: look not behind thee, neither stay thou in the plain; escape to the mountain, lest thou be consumed." (Genesis 19:17)

Lot was able to save his soul by an escape to the mountain, for his "life" would have been lost if he had remained in the area and been "consumed." It is apparent that *nephesh* is subject to death, but the translation obscures this fact, as it does in the next example.

> I and my people were at great strife with the children of Ammon: and when I called you, ye delivered me not out of their hands. And when I saw that ye delivered me not, I put *my life* in my hands, and passed over against the children of

Ammon, and the Lord delivered them into my hand ... (Judges 12:2-3)

In this passage, Jephthah says that he put his *nephesh* "in his hands" when he went up against the children of Ammon; it is apparent that this man feared the loss of his soul in a deadly confrontation with his enemies. That Jephthah wanted to continue on as a "*chay nephesh*" is quite understandable, for when life comes to an end, the "living soul" becomes a dead one:

> Whosoever toucheth *the* dead *body of* any man that is dead, and purifieth not himself, defileth the tabernacle of the Lord. (Numbers 19:13)

> And he that is the high priest among his brethren, upon whose head the anointing oil was poured, and that is consecrated to put on the garments, shall not uncover his head, nor rend his clothes; neither shall he go in to any dead *body*. (Leviticus 21:11)

> Then said Haggai, "If one that is unclean by *a* dead *body* touch any of these, shall it be unclean?" And the priests answered and said, "It shall be unclean." (Haggai 2:13)

Those who come in contact with a corpse are touching a dead soul. A "dead *nephesh*" is a dead person or animal ... a dead life that no longer lives or moves. *Nephesh* is used 13 times to refer to man as being dead, and is always rendered in the *KJV* as "body," "dead body," or "the dead." These translations are, again, unfortunate in that they effectually hide from view the fact that *nephesh* is able to die.

When an Old Testament verse that contains the word *nephesh* is quoted within the Greek New Testament, the word used to represent *nephesh* is *psuche*. It is therefore evident that the Holy Spirit considered these words to have the same meaning, so that both are representative of the English word "soul." (The *nephesh/psuche* relationship may be confirmed by looking up the occurrence of *nephesh* in Psalm 16:10 with a Hebrew Concordance, and *psuche* in Acts 2:27 with a Greek concordance.)

Psuche occurs 105 times in the New Testament and is translated in the *KJV* as "soul" (58 times), "life," and "lives" (40 times), with the remaining as "mind," "you," "heart," "heartily," and "us." A short sample of *psuche* occurrences will demonstrate that the Old Testament definition we have established for "soul" remains consistent throughout the Bible.

> And the third part of the creatures which were in the sea, and had life, died. (Revelation 8:9)

Like *nephesh, psuche* is used in reference to the animals. Here we see that animals *have* soul, or life, whereas Revelation 16:3 demonstrates again that animals *are* souls: "... every living *soul* died in the sea." In the next example, the Apostle Paul reaffirms the teaching we examined in Genesis 2:7.

> And so it is written, "The first man Adam was made a living soul;" the last Adam was made a quickening spirit. (1 Corinthians 15:45)

Again like *nephesh, psuche* is used to describe man at his creation. Below, we see that it is likewise employed to represent a person or persons:

> Then they that gladly received his word were baptized: and the same day there were added unto them about three thousand *souls*. (Acts 2:41)

And in the next verse, from Matthew, *psuche*, too, is a personal pronoun. In this example it is used by God Himself.

> Behold My Servant, Whom I have chosen; My Beloved, in Whom My *soul* is well pleased. (Matthew 12:18)

God uses the word *psuche* in the same manner that *nephesh* was used - with the figure synecdoche, to state that "I am well pleased." In the final examples we see that, also like *nephesh, psuche* is the life of man, and can be lost.

> Arise, and take the young Child and His mother, and go into the land of Israel: for they are dead which sought the young Child's *life*. (Matthew 2:20)

The Christ Child's soul was sought by Herod, who wished "to destroy Him" (verse 13). This verse makes it clear that those who seek a life are seeking to kill soul. The verses below give additional confirmation that *psuche* is mortal:

> Greater love hath no man than this, that a man lay down his *life* for his friends. (John 15:13)
> I am the good Shepherd: the good Shepherd giveth His *life* for the sheep. (John 10:11)

> Greet Priscilla and Aquila my helpers in Christ Jesus: who have for my life laid down their own necks. (Romans 16:3-4)

> He that findeth his *life* shall lose it: and he that loseth his *life* for My sake shall find it. (Matthew 10:39)

Those who lay down their souls for another are subjecting themselves to death. In the Matthew example, we see that a man can lose his *psuche* for the sake of the Lord, i.e., he can die, or give his soul for the witness of Jesus Christ. While the man who "finds" his life in this present world shall lose it utterly, the man who loses his life for Christ's sake shall find it again in resurrection. All Christian people will find that their lives, or their souls, have been saved, for it is God's shining promise that they shall rise again from the dead to experience everlasting life.

> But we are not of them who draw back unto perdition; but of them that believe to the saving of the *soul*. (Hebrews 10:39)

> Wherefore lay apart all filthiness and superfluity of naughtiness, and receive with meekness the engrafted word, which is able to save your *souls*. (James 1:21)

A last point of interest concerning the word *psuche* is the Apostle Paul's use of the derivative *psuchikos* in 1 Corinthians 15:44. Note the contrast of "natural" *(psuchikos),* with "spiritual" *(pneumatikos)*, as Paul explains that there is a difference between our present earthly body and the spiritual body to come:

> It is sown a natural body; it is raised a spiritual body. There is a natural body, and there is a spiritual body. And so it is written, The first man Adam was made a living soul; the last Adam was made a quickening spirit. Howbeit that was not first which is spiritual, but that which is natural; and afterward that which is spiritual. The first man is of the earth, earthy: the second man is the Lord from heaven. As is the earthy, such are they also

that are earthy: and as is the heavenly, such are they also that are heavenly. And as we have borne the image of the earthy, we shall also bear the image of the heavenly. (1 Corinthians 15:44-49)

Paul asserts here that the first body, the one that we are born into, is *psuchikos*; and while there is no word in the English language that directly translates this word, expressions like "soulish" or "soul-ical" are sufficient to convey its meaning. Thus, while the first natural body is "soul-ical," the resurrection body is, in contrast, "spiritual." This is interesting because it demonstrates that the body which is "soulish" – the flesh and blood, "natural," earthy one – is not destined for immortality or eternity.   Rather, we see this body made of dust contrasted with something that *is* truly immortal: the spiritual body of resurrection. This use of *psuchikos,* then, helps to reveal the nature of "soul," and, as "soul" relates to man, it would seem that it is not everlasting, but corruptible. That which is "soulish" does not continue on or transfer to a new body, but it will one day become obsolete, if you will, in favour of that everlasting spiritual body which is to come. For even as we now bear the image of the "earthy" man Adam, we will one day bear the image of the heavenly One, Jesus Christ; for the duration of eternity we shall be "fashioned like unto His glorious body" (Philippians 3:21), and we shall be more like the "quickening spirit" than the earthy "living soul."

The above evidence on the nature of the soul has demonstrated that it is the vital life principle in all living flesh on earth. When the soul, or life, departs the body, God's living, breathing, and moving creature is dead. Simply put, the life is gone and the creature then ceases to be alive and conscious. This is consistent with those scriptures which have described death as "sleep," and which teach a perishing of the thoughts: "in death there is no remembrance of Thee," "the grave cannot praise Thee, death cannot celebrate Thee," (Psalm 6:5, Isaiah 38:18). The departure of life from the body brings man "destruction," "dark(ness)," and "forgetfulness" (Psalm 88:11-12), all of which suggest that man, and his entire "self," comes to an end.

Additionally, it should be noted that *nephesh/psuche/*soul, whether it be used in the sense of the person, the animal, or the life itself, is *always* represented as being mortal. It would seem very curious if, after showing us this mortality repeatedly, the Holy Spirit also intended us to understand the soul as an *im*mortal entity ... and this without ever having committed such a concept to the Scriptures in plain and simple words.

11. What is the spirit?
(*ruach/pneuma*)

The word "spirit" is an English translation of the Hebrew *ruach* in the Old Testament and the Greek *pneuma* in the New Testament. There are many different ways (or senses) in which "spirit" has been used in the Bible, but for the purpose of this study we are interested in one sense only: that which describes the nature of the spirit that inhabits the body of man from birth until death. Whatever sense "spirit" is used in, it always represents that which is invisible to us - God as Spirit, the Holy Spirit, the gifts of the Holy Spirit, angels, breath, wind, a "spirit of meekness," etc.. All we can see of "spirit" are the results of its actions, whether they be physical manifestations, or mental experiences. *Ruach*, which we shall examine first, occurs 389 times, and is usually translated as "spirit," "breath," or "wind" in the *KJV*. It is not until the sixth chapter of Genesis that we find *ruach* referring to man.

> And, behold, I, even I, do bring a flood of waters upon the earth, to destroy all flesh, wherein is *the breath of* life, from under heaven; and everything that is in the earth shall die. (Genesis 6:17)

In this verse, God speaks of His purpose in bringing the great flood upon the earth. The "*ruach* of life," or spirit of life, is said to be within all living flesh,and that would include the flesh of man. The translators choice of the word "breath" is an understandable one, for breath is apparently an outward sign that spirit is contained within:

> All the while my breath is in me, and the spirit of God is in my nostrils...The Spirit of God hath made me, and the breath of the Almighty hath given me life. (Job 27:3, 33:4)

We see that the "*ruach*/spirit of God" imparts the "breath of life" to man, and it is by this breath that he lives. When God breathed the "breath of life" into Adam's nostrils, he became a living soul (Genesis 2:7); the presence of this breath from God was integral to the fact that he was alive.

> Thus saith the Lord God unto these bones; Behold, I will cause *breath* to enter into you, and ye shall live ... Then said He unto me, "Prophesy unto *the wind*, prophesy, son of man, and say to

the wind, Thus saith the Lord God; 'Come from *the* four *winds*, O breath*, and breathe upon these slain, that they may live'" ... "And ye shall know that I am the Lord, when I have opened your graves, O My People, and brought you up out of your graves, and shall put *My spirit* in you, and ye shall live." (Ezekiel 37:5,9,13-14)

These excerpts from Ezekiel's prophetic vision demonstrate to us the basic function of spirit. God puts His *ruach* in man, and this causes man to live. Therefore, it is the eternal spirit of God that is the origin of our life; we have no life-force or eternal spirit of our own. It is also apparent by the Scriptures that the spirit in man is identical to that possessed by the beasts:

For that which befalleth the sons of men befalleth beasts; even one thing befalleth them: as the one dieth, so dieth the other; yea, they have all one *breath*; so that a man hath no preeminence above a beast: for all is vanity. All go unto one place; all are of the dust, and all turn to dust again. (Ecclesiastes 3:19-20)

Man and beast possess the same *ruach*/spirit, for God gives life to both in the same manner. Thus man and beast are alike in body, soul, and spirit, for "all are of the dust," all are "*chay nephesh*," and all have "one *ruach*." The Lord has complete dominion over the spirits contained within His creatures, for He is called "the God of *the spirits* of all flesh" (Numbers 27:16). When the psalmist writes of the beasts great and small, he praises the Lord for His powers of life and death.

Thou takest away *their breath*, they die, and return to their dust. Thou sendest forth *Thy spirit*, they are created: and Thou renewest the face of the earth. (Psalm 104:29-30)

We see again that God's creatures are "created," or made alive, by the sending forth of His own animating spirit into the body of flesh. Note that God's spirit is referred to as "their" spirit (or "breath") while it is yet residing within the living creature. When the spirit, or life-force, leaves the body, death occurs for both man and beast.

If He set His heart upon man, if He gather unto Himself *his spirit* and his breath; all flesh shall perish together, and man shall turn again unto dust. (Job 34:14-15)

Without the spirit and breath that comes from God, man is unable to survive and succumbs to utter death. He has no inherent power to live on his own, and no choice but to enter into "destruction" (Psalm 88: 11):

> *His breath* goeth forth, he returneth to his earth; in that very day his thoughts perish. (Psalm 146:4)

In the very day the *ruach* leaves his body, man's thoughts perish ... and so his consciousness perishes too. It would be accurate for us to look upon death as a "return" to what was before, for the man made of dust becomes dust again, and the spirit that gave him life goes back to its original source.

> Then shall the dust return to the earth as it was: *and the spirit* shall return unto God Who gave it. (Ecclesiastes 12:7)

There is no indication that the spirit that returns to God at death is a conscious, thinking personality. Note that in Psalm 146:4 (above), man is said to "return to his earth," whereas the *ruach* is said to return to the Creator (Ecclesiastes 12:7). Hence, man and the spirit that animated him do not go to the same place when death occurs. And in the case of man, he has been told specifically what to expect at his destination: "there is no work, nor device, nor knowledge, nor wisdom, in the grave, whither thou goest" (Ecclesiastes 9:10).

When a verse that contains the word *ruach* is quoted within the Greek New Testament, the word used to represent *ruach* is *pneuma*. This demonstrates to us that the Holy Spirit considered these two words to have the same exact meaning, so that both are representative of the English word "spirit." (Those readers who have Hebrew and Greek concordances at hand can make a confirming comparison between Joel 2:28-29 and Acts 2:17-18.)

Pneuma is derived from the root word *pneo,* meaning "to blow" or "to breathe," and it occurs 385 times in the New Testament. In the *KJV* it is translated almost exclusively as "Spirit" and "spirit," and coupled with *hagion,* "Holy Spirit" or "Holy Ghost."

While the Old Testament meanings of "spirit" continue on in the New Testament, the word takes on important additional senses with the coming of Christ and the opportunity to be "born again" of the spirit. When one is born again, this does not mean that he, as a spiritual entity, is reborn, for man himself is not a spirit being. A person who is born again is, in a sense, coming alive again in a brand new way because of the entrance of the quickening spirit of God into his heart. Thus, a new spirit, not previously indwelling, takes up residence in the mind of the saint. The Christian becomes newly capable of living "in the spirit" (Romans 8:9), for he receives "*pneuma Christou*" (Christ spirit), and is thus empowered to comprehend the things of God and live his life accordingly (1 John 3:24). A great many of the occurrences of "spirit" in the New Testament are specifically related to the new teachings concerning the indwelling Spirit of Christ; but, the following examples will show that the Old Testament "life-force" sense of "spirit" remains unchanged.

> It is the *spirit* that quickeneth; the flesh profiteth nothing: the words that I speak unto you, they are spirit, and they are life. (John 6:63)

In this first example, Jesus Christ states that the body is lifeless on its own, and that it is quickened, or made alive, by the *pneuma*. He then goes on to compare the spirit which gives life to the body with His own words of the Gospel, (which can quicken us to eternal life). In both instances, it is the spirit of God which makes us alive; like *ruach*, *pneuma* causes man to live.

> And when they shall have finished their testimony, the beast that ascendeth out of the bottomless pit shall make war against them, and shall overcome them, and kill them ... And after three days and an half the *spirit* of life from God entered into them, and they stood upon their feet. (Revelation 11:7,11)

In the prophetic writings of John, we learn that the Lord's two witnesses shall be killed and lay dead for three and a half days. Note again that it is God's *pneuma* which will bring them to life - not a reinstating of their own "immortal spirits." God is "the Father of *spirits*" (Hebrews 12:9) in that He is the origin of all the spirits inhabiting His creatures. When He "taketh away their *ruach*, they die" (Psalm 104:29):

> And they stoned Stephen, calling upon God, and saying, "Lord Jesus, receive my *spirit*." And he kneeled down, and cried with a loud voice, "Lord, lay not this sin to their charge." And when he had said this, he fell asleep. (Acts 7:59-60)

At the time of his stoning, Stephen knew that death was upon him and that his spirit would "return to God Who gave it" (Ecclesiastes 12:7). His words were an acknowledgement of impending death, and after speaking them, he "fell asleep" in Christ. Like *ruach*, *pneuma* describes the inner vitality that makes activity possible. When the *pneuma* leaves the body, the body is no longer alive.

> For as the body without the *spirit* is dead, so faith without works is dead also. (James 2:26)

Here the Apostle James makes a simple comparison between a dead body and a dead faith. Both must be quickened in order to be functional; one by *pneuma*, the other by good works. James states flatly that "the body without the spirit is dead," but if God were to send forth His spirit again, life would return and the body would come alive.

> And He ... took her by the hand, and called, saying, "Maid, arise." And her *spirit* came again, and she arose straightway: and He commanded to give her meat. (Luke 8:54-55)

In this example of resurrection, a young woman was made alive again by the return of her life-bestowing *pneuma*. This divine spirit was "hers" in the sense that it had been given to her to sustain her life for a period of years - just as we saw the spirit of God within the animals referred to as "their spirit" in Psalm 104:29. Thus we may have *pneuma* residing within us for a time, and we may call it "my spirit" as Stephen did, but when our lives are over it returns to "the God of the spirits of all flesh" (Numbers 27:16). While it is correct to say of man that he *has* spirit, it should be noted that the Scriptures have made no reference to him as an "eternal spirit." The phrase "eternal spirit" only occurs once in the entire Bible (Hebrews 9:14), and on this single occasion its use is undoubtedly in reference to God. (As previously noted in the Introduction, the term "immortal spirit" does not occur in the Scriptures at all.)

Before leaving the subject of "spirit," there is one other use of the word which has relevance to the subject at hand. Just as the words "my soul" are sometimes used to indicate "me," "myself," or "I," so also are the words "my spirit" in the case of *ruach* and *pneuma*:

> And the king said unto them, "I have dreamed a dream, and my *spirit* was troubled to know the dream." (Daniel 2:3)

> And Mary said, "My soul doth magnify the Lord, and my *spirit* hath rejoiced in God my Saviour." (Luke 1:46-47)

Both of these examples again demonstrate the use of synecdoche, where an essential aspect of the person is put for the entire being. In the second example, Mary used both *psuche* and *pneuma* in a figurative manner when she spoke to Elizabeth concerning the fruit of her womb. Her intention was to emphasize her great happiness as she herself magnified and rejoiced in God her Saviour.

The collective testimony of the passages above is that spirit/*ruach*/*pneuma* is the life-giving force from our God. It is manifested as the "breath of life" that comes from the Creator, and it returns to Him at death, both in man and beast. When comparing the spirit with the soul in order to mark the difference between the two, they may be thus defined: spirit is that invisible spark from God which animates His creatures, whereas soul is the life which results from that spark. When the spirit goes forth from the body of man at death, the thought process ceases and the person enters the state of "sleep."

It has also been shown that God's creatures are formed of the dust of the earth, and that when death comes upon them, they return to that dust. The particular quality which makes each man an individual personality of his own does not appear to be seated within a separate immortal entity which departs from the body at death. Rather, it would seem that man is a living soul consisting only of dust, and when "he," the person, returns to dust, "he," the person, is thoroughly dead. The Scriptures are worded in such a way as to give many indications that *people* are buried, not just bodies or empty shells; individuality and self are contained within the body, and these all go down to mingle with the dust of the earth when life is over. Therefore, the fact that man has been promised a resurrection from his grave is quite harmonious and truly meaningful. What goes into the grave is "us," and this is precisely what God will bring up out of it.

Finally, having seen "soul" and "spirit" defined plainly in the Bible's words, we can see how unwise it may be to mentally or verbally prefix them with the adjectives "immortal" or "eternal" when they occur in reference to mankind. The resulting catchwords surely serve to radically change both the Bible's intended meanings and our perception of human life.

12. What is hell?
(*sheol/hades*)

Since Scripture does not indicate that there is a conscious entity that survives man's death, we may conclude that the sole path to eternal existence is by the gift of everlasting life, and this only through Jesus Christ. It is evident, then, that the only people to live forever will be God's own righteous ones, and we must therefore question the doctrine of eternal conscious punishment for the unsaved. This we will do by conducting a close examination of pertinent Scriptures; specifically, those which offer insight into the meanings of the Hebrew and Greek words translated as "hell." The story of The Rich Man and Lazarus, which is often used as the foundation of orthodox doctrine concerning hell and Abraham's Bosom, is the most challenging passage of all and has been dealt with as an independent subject in Appendix I.

The word "hell" is an English translation of the Hebrew *sheol* in the *KJV* Old Testament, and the Greek *hades* in the *KJV* New Testament. The Greek word *Gehenna* is also translated as "hell," but since it has a significantly different connotation, it will be investigated separately in the chapter to follow.

Sheol occurs 65 times in the Old Testament and is translated in the *KJV* as "hell" (31 times), "the grave" (31 times), and "pit" (3 times). It is immediately evident that two English words were used almost exclusively in the *KJV* translation, and that these two words are somewhat opposed in meaning: one describes a place of death and corruption, whereas the other describes a place of continuing life. The translators apparently did not settle on a single concept for *sheol*, but instead preferred both, and used their own judgment as to where to use "hell" and where to use "the grave." (In the *NIV* however, *sheol* is never translated "hell", but is represented in the majority of its occurrences by "the grave.") We shall again allow Scripture to define Scripture, learning about *sheol* by the context in which it appears.

The first occurrence is in Genesis 37, where the patriarch Jacob, mourning for his son Joseph, is despondent to the point where he expresses thoughts of dying:

> And all his sons and all his daughters rose up to comfort him; but he refused to be comforted; and he said, "For I will go

down into *the grave* unto my son mourning." Thus his father wept for him. (Genesis 37:35)

Here we see that *sheol* is the place that Jacob expected to "go down into" upon his death. A few chapters later, we find Judah explaining to Joseph that Jacob may again die of sorrow, this time due to the possible loss of Benjamin:

> It shall come to pass, when he seeth that the lad is not with us, that he will die: and thy servants shall bring down the gray hairs of thy servant our father with sorrow *to the grave*. (Genesis 44:31)

Judah speaks of bringing down the "gray hairs" of his father to *sheol*, implying that *sheol* is the place where Jacob's relatives will lay his body after his death. The context shows us that "the grave" is the proper translation here, as does the context in the following example.

> Our bones are scattered at *the grave's* mouth, as when one cutteth and cleaveth wood upon the earth. (Psalm 141:7)

Bones and "the grave" correspond well with each other, suggesting again that *sheol* is the place where bodies are buried. Man's dwelling place after death appears to be a material realm, as the words of Job make evident below:

> If I wait, *the grave* is mine house: I have made my bed in the darkness. I have said to corruption, 'Thou art my father:' to the worm, 'Thou art my mother, and my sister.' And where is now my hope? as for my hope, who shall see it? They shall go down to the bars of *the pit*, when our rest together is in the dust. (Job 17:13-16)

We can see that *sheol* is the place where the sleep of death takes place, for Job speaks of "making his bed" in the darkness of "the grave." His companions in *sheol* will be corruption and the maggot - not the disembodied souls of his loved ones who have died before him. In fact, Job actually refers to corruption and the worm as his relatives, for he knows that they will dwell in intimate togetherness when *sheol* becomes his "house" at the time of his death. The "darkness," "corruption," "worm," and "dust" in this passage imply that Job equates *sheol* with a true and literal grave; the place of destruction. And the references to home and family imply that this grave will be his habitation after death, rather than the traditional spiritual realm. Futhermore, the wording implies that Job himself, his person, expected to dwell there ... not just his dead body. Even his conscious "hope" shall go into corruption, and none "shall see it." As the psalmist below will testify, *sheol* is the place where man decomposes and returns to the dust.

> Man being in honour abideth not: he is like the beasts that perish ... Like sheep they are laid *in the grave*; death shall feed on them; and the upright shall have dominion over them in the morning; and their beauty shall consume in *the grave* from their dwelling. But God will redeem my soul from the power of *the grave*: for He shall receive me. (Psalm 49:12,14-15)

Man does not abide forever, he is like the beasts that perish. Dead animals and dead persons are both laid in *sheol* by human hands. "All go unto one place; all are of the dust, and all turn to dust again" (Ecclesiastes 3:20). Within this grave "death shall feed on them," and "their beauty shall consume," showing again that *sheol* is the place where corruption takes place. After speaking frankly of man's return to dust, however, the psalmist goes on to soften this unpleasant truth with another more happy one: "But God will redeem my *nephesh* (me) from the power of *sheol*." Resurrection is therefore God's answer to the grave's awesome power to retain the dead; for even though death shall bring a man to destruction and the tomb, God shall "buy him back" from *sheol's* domain, and so, one day receive him.

> I have set the Lord always before me: because He is at my right hand, I shall not be moved. Therefore my heart is glad, and my glory rejoiceth: my flesh also shall rest in hope. For Thou wilt not leave my soul *in hell*; neither wilt Thou suffer Thine Holy One to see corruption. Thou wilt shew me the path of life: in Thy presence is fulness of joy. (Psalm 16:8-11)

Although the translators chose to use the word "hell" in this passage, we can see that its subject is essentially similar to Psalm 49 above. If we read instead, "for Thou wilt not leave me in the grave," we are easily able to see David's faith in the promise of resurrection. When he dies he will "rest in hope," knowing that the Lord will not leave him in *sheol* - he, and the Holy One also, will be redeemed from "the grave" to live again.

That the Holy One would not "see corruption" in *sheol* is very interesting, and indicates that the verse is speaking of the physical body of the Lord. The presence of the word "corruption" signals us that "the grave" is the correct meaning of *sheol*, for bodies are subject to corruption, and bodies lie in the grave. After His crucifixion, the Lord's body lay in *sheol* for three days, yet He did not suffer decomposition, but was raised from the dead. Likewise, David knew that he too would not be left in the grave forever, but will one day be shown "the path of life."

It is fitting, then, that when the Lord Himself makes the promise of resurrection, He simultaneously vows to bring an end to the reign of death. Note that when God speaks of death and *sheol*, He represents them as a pair of powerful adversaries ... enemies to be destroyed and defeated.

> I will ransom them from the power of the grave; I will redeem them from death: O death, I will be thy plagues; O grave, I will be thy destruction. (Hosea 13:14)

The "power of the grave" to retain its inhabitants is evidenced by the fact that the dead have helplessly dissolved into dust. Those who are in *sheol* are deeply entrapped within its restrictive grasp. Thus, it will take an even greater power - the Lord's power of resurrection - to ransom or redeem men from the tenacious state of death. Although the redeemed man will enter into a period of destruction in *sheol*, there is a time and a season when he shall emerge again in glory.

> So man lieth down and riseth not; till the heavens be no more, they shall not awake, nor be raised out of their sleep. O that Thou wouldest hide me *in the grave*, that Thou wouldest keep me secret, until Thy wrath be past, that Thou wouldest appoint me a set time, and remember me! If a man die, shall he live again? all the days of my appointed time will I wait, till my change come. (Job 14:12-14)

Job informs us that man will not "awake" from his sleep in *sheol* until "the heavens be no more." It seems obvious that he had some knowledge of the great tribulation to come, for he apparently makes reference to what later became known as the opening of the sixth seal: "the stars of heaven fell unto the earth" and "the heaven departed as a scroll when it is rolled together" (Revelation 6:12-14, Matthew 24:29-30). Thus it appears that man will remain dead in *sheol* until the day of the Lord, or, as we have seen, the second coming of Jesus Christ. (And if he remains sleeping in *sheol* until resurrected, then it is not possible for him to be in a heavenly paradise with the Lord at any time prior to this event - see Luke 23:43, Appendix II.) Job speaks of waiting in the grave until he is "remembered," and when he wakes up he will come forth from *sheol* with a new and incorruptible body. His hope of living again shall not be realized until his "appointed time" in the grave is finished - when the Lord Jesus Christ raises him up at the last day.

While *sheol* is evidently **a** grave, it has the deeper connotation of being **the** grave. It represents the state of death in much the same way that "sleep" does, only its use is less poetic and analogous, and more to the point. The Holy Spirit has taught us that death is like sleep, but He also wishes us to recognize the grim reality that death is epitomized by the grave - that dark and silent place where our bodies turn to dust. *Sheol* is therefore never represented as the kind of place that a contented man would rejoice to arrive at. Even a cursory look at the occurrences of *sheol* would reveal that men wished to avoid entry for as long as possible ... not because it is a prison or a flaming pit, but because it is a dark "land of forgetfulness" (Psalm 88:11-12) where all consciousness comes to an end.

Now the contexts of the passages presented thus far in this chapter have provided some very strong evidence for the conclusion that *sheol* is indeed "the grave." While the *KJV* translators were often constrained by the contexts to choose "the grave" as their rendition, they took many opportunities to render *sheol* as "hell" - an English word which describes a nether world of "eternal souls." This assignment of a dual definition to *sheol* is indicative of the more popular and traditional interpretations of the word. Many believe that it has always possessed two distinct meanings, rather than one: "the grave," (or death state), and a spiritual realm of "the next life." Others view *sheol* as a spiritual realm only, suggesting that the early men of God sometimes perceived and wrote about it from the standpoint of the "natural" earthbound man ... a "human standpoint" which led them to write of *sheol* as if it were the equivalent of the grave. And, some scholars have alternatively theorized that the ancients appear to have believed in utter death and destruction because they were, in fact, totally ignorant about the nature of the death state. This proposal postulates that there is indeed continuous life after death, but that God did not reveal to early men, thereby explaining why they reasoned and wrote of *sheol* as it were merely the tomb. Thus, today's most prevailing points of view assert that - either by God's intention or through man's use of a "human standpoint" - the word *sheol* came to be used to describe both the place of corruption *and* a spiritual realm.

But that early man might have been ignorant about death seems unthinkable, for how could it happen that he would be so fully enlightened about the promise of resurrection, without also being enlightened as to what state he would be resurrected from? (How likely does it seem that God would give man the hope of rising again from death without even telling him what his death consists of?) Since Job, for instance, knew about the promise of life, and also knew when it would be granted, it is reasonable that we should count him as knowledgeable about the death state, as well. If godly men such as he were simply writing from ignorance or "the human standpoint" when they wrote of death's utter destruction, we might ask to what purpose God would have them do this, and with such repetition throughout the Old Testament? Why inspire David to write, in the midst of a songful prayer, "in death there is no remembrance of Thee," if this be not the truth? It is difficult to imagine that God would be the author of such confusion. And indeed, confusion would reign if it were true that *sheol* possessed a double meaning by divine intention, as some will maintain: in such a case men of God would be left continually guessing as to which meaning was intended in each of the 65 occurrences.

If we trust that the ancients have written the truth about death as it was revealed to them by God, then there is no need to utilize such dual understandings of *sheol*; "the grave," by itself, can be acknowledged as the one correct definition. And when *sheol* is recognized to be "the grave," and nothing else, we find that such a meaning enables it to sit in complete harmony with the Biblical mortality of soul and the proclaimed wages of sin - for "the grave" is where we all must go to meet the devastating penalty of death. Furthermore, "the grave" makes reasonable sense in every one of *sheol's* occurrences, so that the integrity of God's word is by no means compromised. Thus, whereas some of the following passages may lend themselves to the interpretation that *sheol* is an underworld for souls, we can also see that "the grave" is always a workable and meaningful translation.

> Let not thine heart decline to her ways, go not astray in her paths. For she hath cast down many wounded: Yea, many strong men have been slain by her. Her house is the way to hell, going down to the chambers of death. (Proverbs 7:25-27)

Note that the given direction of *sheol* is down, just as the place of interment is. When we alter the translation to read that the foreign woman's house is "the way to the grave," there is no disturbance within the verses - many strong men have been "slain" by her, and the "chambers of death" comes across as an apt description of the tomb. The proverb thus provides a simple reminder that sin will lead to death and the grave ... a law which would also seem to apply to Satan, as the passage below suggests.

> How art thou fallen from heaven, O Lucifer, son of the morning! ... For thou hast said in thine heart, 'I will ascend into heaven, I will exalt my throne above the stars of God ... I will ascend above the heights of the clouds; I will be like the Most High.' Yet thou shalt be brought down to hell, to the sides of the pit. (Isaiah 14:12-15)

Even as death is the fate of all those in Adam, so it is also promised to the wicked cherub who sinned (Ezekiel 28:11-19). When "the grave" is substituted for "hell" in this passage, there is no loss of sense; Satan shall be brought down to death and destruction, that the root of sin might be cut off forever. When we take note of the word "pit" at the close of the passage, we find that it is the Hebrew *bor*, meaning a sepulchre hewn from stone. Thus, Satan is to be brought to the edge of the *burial* pit, which would be an odd thing for God to declare unless He intended to totally destroy him. (It is possible that bringing Satan "to the grave, to the sides of the pit" may be figurative speech that only infers destruction, not burial. For Ezekiel 28:11-19, which obviously refers to an extra-terrestrial being who can only be Satan, is more specific:" ... I will bring forth a fire from the midst of thee, it shall devour thee, and I will bring thee to ashes upon the earth ... thou shalt be a terror, and never shalt thou be anymore" (verses 18-19). It doesn't appear that there will be much left to bury, but an end, or destruction, is clearly certain here. Some would even link this divinely generated "fire" to the visionary lake into which Satan is cast in Revelation.) In the next example, we can again perceive that *sheol* is "the grave" as we consider the account of the rebellion of Korah:

> The ground clave asunder that was under them: and the earth opened her mouth, and swallowed them up, and their houses, and all the men that appertained unto Korah, and all their goods. They, and all that appertained to them, went down alive *into the pit*, and the earth closed upon them: and they perished from among the congregation. (Numbers 16:31-33)

Men, cattle, tents, etc., went into *sheol* when "the earth opened her mouth, and swallowed them up". When we recognize that *sheol* is "the grave," it becomes clear that the rebels were simply buried alive in a mass tomb when the ground "clave asunder." But if *sheol* is recognized as a spiritual realm here, we must surely question the apparent entrance of flesh and household goods. (For it would seem odd if the material corpses of man and beast were presumed to be decomposing within a spiritual realm. And, in addition, a further line of reasoning would seem to dictate that the spiritually conscious individual would then be in the position of observing the decay of his own body.) In this case from Numbers, "the grave" is certainly a less complicated rendering than "hell" would be. Also simplified is the 86th Psalm below, where David is praising the mercy of his God:

> For great is Thy mercy toward me: and Thou hast delivered my soul from the lowest *hell*. O God, the proud are risen against me, and the assemblies of violent men have sought after my soul. (Psalm 86:13-14)

While this passage may seem to suggest that there is a multi-level subterranean abode for men's "eternal souls," the substitution of "the grave" for "hell" continues to be a workable translation. The Lord had delivered David from "the lowest *sheol*," or the deepest grave: words which are figuratively put for what seemed like his certain death. This rendition is supported by the verse which follows, for "the assemblies of violent men have sought after my *nephesh*/life." Thus, while David's life was sought by his enemies, his God delivered him from death and "the grave."

Our next passage, from Isaiah, is especially notable in that the dead appear to speak from within the depths of *sheol*. The passage tells of *sheol* being moved and stirring up the dead, who then call out to the King of Babylon and taunt him about his impending death:

> The whole earth is at rest, and is quiet: they break forth into singing. Yea, the fir trees rejoice at thee, and the cedars of Lebanon, saying, 'Since thou art laid down, no feller is come up against us.' *Hell* from beneath is moved for thee to meet thee at thy coming: it stirreth up the dead for thee, even all the chief ones of the earth; it hath raised up from their thrones all the kings of the nations. All they shall speak and say unto thee, 'Art thou also become weak as we? art thou become like unto us?' Thy pomp is brought down to *the grave*, and the noise of thy viols: the worm is spread under thee, and the worms cover thee. (Isaiah 14:7-11)

When considering whether the dead can actually speak, we must also consider whether the cedar and fir trees are able to speak, for they, too, are given voice here. Seeing this, we can deduce that the figure of speech personification is being used: the application of intelligence, by actions or words, to inanimate objects or abstract concepts. When *sheol* is translated as "the grave" in both of its occurrences here, there is no distortion of meaning. We see the dead in "the grave" figuratively calling out to the King of Babylon, mockingly the proclaiming the impotence he will experience when he joins them among the worms. These "worms" strongly suggest a literal grave rather than a spiritual realm, so that we wonder at why the translators chose to use "hell" in this passage at all.

Also of interest is the next example, which will allow the reader to view *sheol* from a slightly different aspect. While our former passages have given clues about *sheol's* location and function, we shall now glimpse the godly man's attitude towards his certain destination at death.

> I love the Lord, because He hath heard my voice and my supplications. Because He hath inclined His ear unto me, therefore will I call upon Him as long as I live. The sorrows of death compassed me, and the pains of *hell* gat hold upon me: I found trouble and sorrow. Then I called upon the Lord; O Lord, I beseech Thee, deliver my soul ... Return unto thy rest, O my soul; for the Lord hath dealt bountifully with thee. For Thou hast delivered my soul from death, mine eyes from tears, and my feet from falling. I will walk before the Lord in the land of the living. (Psalm 116:1-4,7-9)

This prayer of thanksgiving rejoices in the fact that its author was saved from *sheol*. His distaste for death is apparent, but especially notable is his sensation of "the pains of hell." When we substitute "the grave" in place of "hell" in this passage, there is again no loss of sense. The man is found to be rejoicing because he has been delivered from "the sorrows of death" and the "pains of the grave"... a figurative way of expressing the pain of death itself. The psalmist is happy and thankful because he remains alive in "the land of the living," where he is actually able to call upon the Lord. Without understanding *sheol* as "the grave" in this passage, we are confronted with a man of God who was truly expecting discomfort in "hell." If *sheol* is understood to be a spiritual realm here, the resulting implication of the full passage would be that the godly man could expect pain and sorrow in his "afterlife" ... a state of affairs that is traditionally attributed to the unredeemed. But when *sheol* is recognized as "the grave," we realize that all men find the same thing within its domain. They go to a place where there is absolutely nothing, and all that confronts them is the vast emptiness of death:

> Whatsoever thy hand findeth to do, do it with thy might; for there is no work, nor device, nor knowledge, nor wisdom, in *the grave*, whither thou goest. (Ecclesiastes 9:10)

Sheol represents the state of destruction, a condition in which man no longer possesses any consciousness or being. When *sheol* occurs in the context of the fate of the unredeemed, we encounter no difficulty when we consistently translate "the grave." Thus, when the psalmist declares that "the wicked shall be turned into hell," (Psalm 9:17), we understand this to mean that the grave is their punishment; the penalty of sin is death without redemption, and the wicked shall spend their eternity as dust.

When a verse that contains the word *sheol* is quoted within the Greek New Testament, the word used to represent *sheol* is *hades*. Those who have Hebrew and Greek concordances can confirm this relationship by making a comparison between Psalm 16:10 and Acts 2:27. *Hades* occurs only eleven times in the New Testament and is translated in the *KJV* as "hell" ten times, and "grave" once. (Note that in the *NIV* it is translated "Hades" 5 times, "depths" twice, and "hell" once.) Since the occurrences of *hades* are so few, and because their contexts offer little additional information which would help to define the word, it is logical that we should apply the previously established definition of *sheol* to its Greek equivalent. When *hades* is recognized as "the grave," many of the passages in which it appears take on more clarity, especially when resurrection is contained within the context. The first occurrence, from the Gospel of Matthew, is a simple statement of judgment by the Lord Jesus Christ:

> And thou, Capernaum, which art exalted unto heaven, shalt be brought down to *hell*. (Matthew 11:23)

Here the Lord is upbraiding one of the cities that did not repent, condemning its people to death and the grave. Since we know that the wages of sin is death, "the grave" makes sense as the final destination of those who do not "have life" in the Son of God. In the next example, the Apostle Peter quotes from David's Psalm 16, which we have only just examined under the heading of *sheol*. When Peter explains that

David was speaking of "the resurrection of Christ" in his psalm, it can be seen that Peter, too, regarded *hades* to be "the grave."

> "'Thou wilt not leave my soul in *hell*, neither wilt thou suffer Thine Holy One to see corruption'... (David) spake of the resurrection of Christ, that His soul was not left in *hell*, neither His flesh did see corruption." (Acts 2:27,31)

Like *sheol*, *hades* is employed to describe the "place" where corruption of the flesh occurs. When we substitute "the grave" for "hell" in these verses, there is no loss of intelligibility; rather, the already present resurrection theme is strengthened. The Lord was not left to decay in *hades*/the grave, but was resurrected to life after three days and three nights. All others who enter "the grave" have seen corruption, as Peter informs us that David did.

> For David, after he had served his own generation by the will of God, fell on sleep, and was laid unto his fathers, and saw corruption. But He, Whom God raised again, saw no corruption. (Acts 13:36-37)

Thus, the Lord "was not left in *hell*," but David apparently remains there even now, "for David is not ascended into the heavens" (Acts 2:34). This is perfectly agreeable with the concept that the Lord has been made alive again from the grave, but that no other person has yet seen life. When the proper season arrives, and the Lord *does* raise His faithful from the dead, He has promised that "the gates of *hades*" shall not prevail against them:

> And I say also unto thee, That thou art Peter, and upon this rock I will build My church; and the gates of *hell* shall not prevail against it. (Matthew 16:18)

These words take on a fresh and deeper meaning when we understand *hades* to be "the grave." The underlying subject is revealed to be the promise of resurrection, with the Lord again referring to the power of the grave to retain the dead. This power is symbolized by the figure of a closed gate, and the same expression can also be seen in Isaiah 38:10. But the "gates of the grave" which have closed tight on the sleeping shall not remain forever shut. They shall be opened by a power which exceeds the grave's power, thus enabling the faithful to exit into life and immortality. When Jesus Christ returns to the earth, He shall unlock the gates for He is the one in possession of the key:

I am He That liveth, and was dead; and behold, I am alive for evermore, Amen; and have the keys of *hell* and of death. (Revelation 1:18)

This verse from Revelation has the imminently returning Jesus Christ speaking to John within his end-time vision. At the moment that the words are spoken, the Lord is still the only One Who is alive beyond death, and He identifies Himself to John by this great distinction. When *hades* is translated as "the grave" here, there is again no distortion of meaning, and the resurrection of the saints comes to the forefront at the Lord's imminent return. His appearance with "the keys" implies that He will soon use them to fulfil His promises of opening the graves and destroying the grip of death. When His people are finally raised and transformed to life and immortality, *hades* will be brought down in a crushing defeat.

So when this corruptible shall have put on incorruption, and this mortal shall have put on immortality, then shall be brought to pass the saying that is written, "Death shall be swallowed up in victory." "O death, where is thy sting? O *grave*, where is thy victory?" The sting of death is sin; and the strength of sin is the law. But thanks be to God, Which giveth us the victory through our Lord Jesus Christ. (1 Corinthians 15:54-58)

The resurrection and transformation of the saints are Christianity's great triumphs over death and *hades*. Our great joy is that we will be rescued from our graves and from the mighty dominion of death - for without this rescue, death would reign on eternally. Thus Paul quotes from the Hosea 13:14 passage that we saw previously, and which also says, "I will ransom them from the power of *the grave*; I will redeem them from death." *Hades* is the natural destination of all men, including the members of the church to whom Paul was writing here. Only when we "put on immortality" through resurrection or transformation will we be forever free of its reaching grasp.

Our final examples of *hades* are all to be found in Revelation, the written account of John's surrealistic vision concerning the end-time. Here the student finds himself in the difficult position of trying to separate literal reality from visionary figures that merely *represent* reality. *Hades* as "the grave" poses no problems within this book, but instead remains sensible and relevant when the contexts are examined with this point of view.

And I looked, and behold, a pale horse: and his name that sat on him was Death, and *Hell* followed with him. And power was given unto them over the fourth part of the earth, to kill with sword, and with hunger, and with death, and with the beasts of the earth. (Revelation 6:8)

Death and *hades* are personified in this verse, and their intimate connection is very evident: death is followed by "the grave." Power was given unto "them" to kill by physical means, and it is apparent that they will take quite a toll during the tribulation to come. "The grave" comes across as a very adequate translation of *hades* in this occurrence, for the state of true death in the tomb is easily perceived to possess the "killing power" that is mentioned. But "hell," as a spiritual realm, may be a little out of place here, for it is ever notorious not for killing, but for preserving life.

The next quotation is taken from John's description of the second resurrection, at which time Death and Hades will be given yet another task. The *KJV* does not continue to capitalize "death" and "hell," but since they are initially introduced as personified figures, there is good reason to continue to perceive them as such.

And the sea gave up the dead which were in it; and death and *hell* delivered up the dead which were in them: and they were judged every man according to their works. (Revelation 20:13)

When *hades* is recognized to be "the grave" in this verse, we see that the apostle is speaking of resurrection *from* the grave *to* judgment, as was prophesied in John 5:28-29. Dead men are sleeping in the dust of their graves, and at resurrection they will come forth from their tombs - not from a paradise, or a spiritual realm. The sea will also deliver up the dead since, for some people, the sea is "the grave" rather than the dust of the earth. Whatever the case for each man, *hades* is the place where the dead remain up until the time of their resurrection ... after they have been removed, Death and Hell shall meet with their fate.

And death and *hell* were cast into the lake of fire. This is the second death. (Revelation 20:14)

This final verse announces the destruction of death and "the grave," as previously promised in Hosea 13:14 and 1 Corinthians 15:26. These two enemies shall have no part to play in the eternal world to come, for their destruction in the lake conveys the permanent end of death and the permanent end of *sheol/hades*. After the final lake events, no one will die, no one will enter the grave, and no one will ever again come out of it. Resurrection will be over, and all those remaining in *sheol/ hades* shall be shut within its "gates" forever.

It is not difficult to see that "the grave" is a workable and meaningful translation of *sheol* and *hades*, even within the Bible's many various contexts. If we acknowledge that the ancient writers of Scripture were fully enlightened about the death state - and gave a correct representation of its emptiness - we may conclude that "the grave" is the one true definition of these words. From the Biblical description given by men of God, *sheol/hades* is the place where corpses are laid and consumed by corruption. Its given direction is down, and from all accounts we can approximate that it is under the earth. While many have suggested and taught that it is a place of life after death, no writer of scripture has actually said so in plain words. As we continue on in our study we will find confirmation that the Godless will spend eternity in this place, in true death and non-existence; but the Lord will show His faithful ones the "path of life" spoken of by David.

The English word "hell," therefore, would appear to have a very different meaning than that of *sheol* or *hades*, and for this reason many Christians have declined to use it as an equivalent for these Hebrew and Greek words. "Hell" is invariably understood by others as a spiritual realm inhabited by immortal souls - a far different concept from "*the grave*" where "the worm is spread under thee, and the worms cover thee" (Isaiah 14:11). Man's belief in his own immortality has led him to conclude that when he goes down into *sheol/hades*, he must be consciously entering a subterranean world; but when mortality is acknowledged, and death is realized to be complete, the evidential conclusion is that man is simply descending into his own grave.

13. Hell and hell fire (*Ge Hinnom/Gehenna*)

We have just seen that *sheol/hades* represents the state of death in the grave, and that it holds no expectation of conscious awareness for the dead. Our next task is to investigate *Gehenna*, a Greek word which is also translated as "hell" in the *KJV* New Testament, and which frequently occurs within the context of fire. With the exception of one recorded use by the Apostle James (James 3:6), the Biblical occurrences of *Gehenna* are exclusive to Jesus Christ during His earthly ministry to Israel. But before we can fully understand how and why the Lord used this particular word, we must first turn back to the Old Testament to discover its meaning.

Gehenna is a transliteration into Greek of the Hebrew *Ge Hinnom*, meaning "valley (of) Hinnom." Therefore, both of these words simply represent the proper name of a geographical location, easily found on any map of ancient Jerusalem. The Bible's first mention of *Ge Hinnom* occurs in the book of Joshua, where the inheritance in the land of Canaan is distributed to the Israelites. Here we see the valley used simply as a landmark in describing the lot of the tribe of Judah.

> And the border went up by the valley of the son of Hinnom unto the south side of the Jebusite; the same is Jerusalem: and the border went up to the top of the mountain that lieth before the valley of Hinnom westward, which is at the end of the valley of the giants northward. (Joshua 15:8)

The "valley of Hinnom," (also called the valley of the son of Hinnom), was the name given to the junction of three valleys that unite south of Jerusalem. It eventually became the site of Tophet, where high altars were constructed in order to facilitate idolatrous worship:

> For the children of Judah have done evil in My sight, saith the Lord: they have set their abominations in the house which is called by My name, to pollute it. And they have built the high places of Tophet, which is in the valley of the son of Hinnom, to burn their sons and their daughters in the fire; which I commanded them not, neither came it into My heart. Therefore, behold, the days come, saith the Lord, that it shall no more be called Tophet, nor the valley of the son of Hinnom, but the

valley of slaughter: for they shall bury in Tophet, till there be no place. (Jeremiah 7:30-32)

Here we see that *Ge Hinnom* was used for the offering of human sacrifice, and that fire was the method by which the People destroyed their children. Also of interest is the origin of the word "Tophet," which is a transliteration of the Hebrew *topteh*, meaning "burning place." Thus, a relationship between *Ge Hinnom* and fire is plainly established. Some additional information can be gathered further on in Jeremiah, when the Lord speaks again by the mouth of His prophet.

> Thus saith the LORD, Go and get a potter's earthen bottle, and take of the ancients of the people, and of the ancients of the priests; And go forth unto the valley of the son of Hinnom, which is by the entry of the east gate, and proclaim there the words that I shall tell thee, And say, Hear ye the word of the LORD, O kings of Judah, and inhabitants of Jerusalem; Thus saith the LORD of hosts, the God of Israel; Behold, I will bring evil upon this place, the which whosoever heareth, his ears shall tingle. Because they have forsaken Me, and have estranged this place, and have burned incense in it unto other gods, whom neither they nor their fathers have known, nor the kings of Judah, and have filled this place with the blood of innocents; They have built also the high places of Baal, to burn their sons with fire for burnt offerings unto Baal, which I commanded not, nor spake it, neither came it into my mind; therefore, behold, the days come, saith the LORD, that this place shall no more be called Tophet, nor The valley of the son of Hinnom, but The valley of slaughter. And I will make void the counsel of Judah and Jerusalem in this place; and I will cause them to fall by the sword before their enemies, and by the hands of them that seek their lives; and their carcases will I give to be meat for the fowls of the heaven, and for the beasts of the earth. And I will make this city desolate, and an hissing; every one that passeth thereby shall be astonished and hiss because of all the plagues thereof.' ... Then shalt thou break the bottle in the sight of the men that go with thee, and shalt say unto them, 'Thus saith the LORD of hosts; Even so will I break this people and this city, as one breaketh a potter's vessel, that cannot be made whole again: and they shall bury them in Tophet, till there be no place to bury.'"(Jeremiah 19:1-8,10-11)

Through Jeremiah's prophecy, Hinnom became associated with judgment, because it is mentioned as the place where God's judgment will fall. Death and destruction are apparent consequences, as God has threatened to break both "this People and this city." The Israelites are said to have "filled this place with the blood of innocents," giving their children as "burnt offerings" to Baal (see also 32:35). God's displeasure at their behavior is quite obvious, and *Ge Hinnom* itself is called "estranged" by the dishonorable acts that took place on its soil.

Incredibly, the evil of child sacrifice was practiced even by some of Israel's kings (2 Chronicles 28:3, 33:6). But 2 Kings 23:1-25 details an act of reformation in which King Josiah defiled Tophet, "that no man might make his son or his daughter to pass through the fire to Molech" (verse 10). He destroyed the entire area with its altars, images, and groves, and he executed the idolatrous priests, filling the "high places" with the bones of men. This act rendered the site unclean, (as a place of the dead), and occurred at approximately 625 B.C.. The fiery sacrifices came to an end, but *Ge Hinnom* remained notorious as a place of much shame and disgrace.

Many scholars agree that by the time of the writing of the Gospels, the Valley of Hinnom had long been used as the dumping ground for the offal of the city of Jerusalem. Since the carcasses of animals used for food would have been dumped there, as well as rubbish, fires would have burned continually to prevent the spread of disease. Of particular interest is the probability that the corpses of dishonored lawbreakers would have been thrown there as well, for such individuals were denied burial. In New Testament times, then, the fire of *Ge Hinnom* was not only a haunting fire of the past, but likely also a literal one which consumed and destroyed the unwanted refuse of Jerusalem.

While the Hebrew *Ge Hinnom* is always translated in a manner which adequately represents it as the name of a geographical location, the New Testament translation of the Greek *Gehenna* is sadly lacking. The fact that a valley surrounding Jerusalem to its south should be rendered by the translators as "hell" - rather than by its proper name - seems very curious, and perhaps reveals a bias toward the traditional beliefs. Only God knows whether the translators simply failed to recognize *Gehenna* as the transliteration of *Ge Hinnom*, or whether they deliberately chose to suppress the actual landmark in order to obscure the true origin of the Lord's judgment fire. Perhaps their motive was simply to insure that subsequent readers would see things in the same light they did. Whatever the case, the result has been confusion for God's people, and

Gehenna continues to remain synonymous with the English meaning of "hell."

Gehenna occurs 12 times in the New Testament and is rendered by the *KJV* translators as "hell" on every one of these occasions. The context is always one of judgment and/or destruction, and the speaker is, (with the one exception already mentioned), always the Lord Jesus Christ.

> Ye have heard that it was said by them of old time, 'Thou shalt not kill; and whosoever shall kill shall be in danger of the judgment:' but I say unto you, That whosoever is angry with his brother without a cause shall be in danger of the judgment: and whosoever shall say to his brother, 'Raca,' shall be in danger of the council: but whosoever shall say, 'Thou fool,' shall be in danger of *hell* fire. (Matthew 5:21-22)

In this first New Testament reference to the valley, the Lord is addressing His disciples in "The Sermon on the Mount." A literal translation of the Greek would read, "liable shall be to the *Gehenna* of fire," and when we recognize that the Lord is referring to Hinnom, there is no compelling need to visualize the traditional eternal hell. The threat here is of the valley's fire, which the Lord uses symbolically to invoke mental images of shame and dishonor; and fire itself, which typically destroys whatever is put into it, portends the woeful judgment of death that will surely come upon the unredeemed. Thus, persons who are "in danger of *Gehenna* fire" are in danger of destruction, a concept which can also be seen in the contexts of the passages to follow.

> And if thy right eye offend thee, pluck it out, and cast it from thee: for it is profitable for thee that one of thy members should perish, and not that thy whole body should be cast into *hell*. And if thy right hand offend thee, cut it off, and cast it from thee: for it is profitable for thee that one of thy members should perish, and not that thy whole body should be cast into *hell*. (Matthew 5:29-30)

At this point in the same Sermon, the Lord indicates that it would be better to cut off the member that commits a transgression, rather than to have the whole body perish in the valley of Hinnom; thus, the warning implies that the entire person of the unredeemed shall be destroyed, whereas only parts of the righteous will perish if they remove the offending member. The Lord's words are obviously figurative here, but the underlying message is evident. The Valley again used shrewdly to represent an appropriate fate for the unredeemed. The disgrace of an "end" in *Gehenna* was undoubtedly an ominous thought for the Lord's audience; and the valley of fire and infamy made a fitting symbol of destruction for those who would not love the commandments of God. In the next example, the teaching on removing the offensive member is reiterated, with *Gehenna* made even more menacing by the Lord's use of the words "everlasting fire."

> Woe unto the world because of offences! for it must needs be that offences come; but woe to that man by whom the offence cometh! Wherefore if thy hand or thy foot offend thee, cut them off, and cast them from thee: it is better for thee to enter into life halt or maimed, rather than having two hands or two feet to be cast into everlasting fire. And if thine eye offend thee, pluck it out, and cast it from thee: it is better for thee to enter into life with one eye, rather than having two eyes to be cast into *hell* fire. (Matthew 18:7-9)

In this passage we can see that the basic alternatives are either to "enter into life," or to be cast into *Gehenna* fire (i.e., "not see life," John 3:36). The flames of Hinnom are again used to describe destruction, and while they are said to be everlasting in nature, there is no indication that the persons cast into them will somehow live eternally within the blaze. Fire, by nature, consumes and destroys, and this fire may be everlasting in the simple sense that its dreadful consequences will be permanent and irreversible: it burns forever, and so destroys forever. Thus, the Lord states that it is better to enter into everlasting life maimed, than to enter whole into the fire which results in everlasting destruction. There is one more instance in which this particular teaching occurs, and while it may seem repetitious to quote it here, it will further our understanding of the Lord's use of Hinnom.

> And if thy hand offend thee, cut it off: it is better for thee to enter into life maimed, than having two hands to go into *hell*, into the fire that never shall be quenched: where their worm dieth not, and the fire is not quenched. And if thy foot offend thee, cut it off: it is better for thee to enter halt into life, than having two feet to be cast into *hell*, into the fire that never shall be quenched: where their worm dieth not, and the fire is not quenched. And if thine eye offend thee, pluck it out: it is better for thee to enter into the kingdom of God with one eye, than having two eyes to be cast into *hell* fire: where their worm dieth not, and the fire is not quenched. (Mark 9:43-48)

In these verses, Christ repeats the threat of *Gehenna* fire, and He emphasizes His lesson by quoting a portion of Isaiah three times. Turning back to Isaiah's prophecy, we read,

> And they shall go forth, and look upon the carcases of the men that have transgressed against Me: for their worm shall not die, neither shall their fire be quenched; and they shall be an abhorring unto all flesh. (Isaiah 66:24)

This closing verse to the book of Isaiah states that the godly will one day go forth and gaze repugnantly upon the "carcases" of those who transgressed against God. In quoting this verse repeatedly in the Mark 9 passage above, the Lord links *Gehenna* with the dead bodies of the unredeemed. This strongly suggests that He intended the valley to symbolize the execution and destruction of flesh and blood, rather than the eternal conscious punishment of incorruptible spiritual bodies. The presence of "worms" in these passages would seem to confirm this, for the maggot is associated strictly with the natural decomposition process that begins after death. The worm that does "not die," but eats forever, can easily symbolize a perpetual fate within *sheol*, the grave; and the fire that shall never be quenched, but burns forever, can portray an everlasting destruction with no hope of reversal. Thus, the Lord's use of *Gehenna* can be interpreted as the symbolic "place" that the unsaved will meet their doom, with its flames depicting the destruction of the living, not the everlasting torment of the spiritually dead. While Christ's words are doubtlessly artful and threatening, they do not necessarily imply the popular concept of eternal hell. As we shall see more clearly in the example to follow, those who are cast into *Gehenna* shall be completely destroyed.

> And fear not them which kill the body, but are not able to kill the soul: but rather fear Him Which is able to destroy both soul and body in *hell*. (Matthew 10:28)

Here we see that God is able to destroy both body and *psuche* in *Gehenna* - a capability that He will surely exercise towards those who do not seek righteousness. As we have already seen prior examples which show that a man can indeed kill soul (in the sense of taking a life), we can deduce that in this verse the Lord is probably referring to the soul as "the person." Man can kill his brother and cause death and decomposition, but he cannot forever destroy another man's self: life can be restored to the dead through the power of resurrection. God wields the ultimate decision of eternal life or death, and it is He Who should be feared - not man - for He alone can truly implement permanent human destruction by electing to withhold everlasting life. And, indeed, the statement that God is able to "destroy" body and soul in *Gehenna* implies that the disciples should fear destruction in this "place"... not eternal conscious punishment.

> "Fear Him, Which after He hath killed hath power to cast into *Gehenna*" (Luke 12:5).

For, once a man is subjected to the utter destruction that *Gehenna* stands for, he is gone for eternity; its symbolic ever-burning and ever-destroying fire shall continually overrule the possibility of his resurrection from the grave.

The Lord's final two uses of *Gehenna* are found within His Matthew 23 address to the multitude at the temple. On this occasion He uttered a series of denouncements, or "woes," which were directed at the Pharisees, and in particular, at their practices. In the passage below we see just one accusation in what was a scathing criticism of Israel's most prominent sect.

> Woe unto you, scribes and Pharisees, hypocrites! for ye compass sea and land to make one proselyte, and when he is made, ye make him twofold more the child of *hell* than yourselves ...Ye serpents, ye generation of vipers, how can ye escape the damnation of *hell*? (Matthew 23:15,33)

In calling the Pharisees (literally) "sons of *Gehenna*," the Lord was both condemning their evil works and warning them of the judgment to come. In view of what went on at Hinnom in the years past, the appellation "child of Gehenna" was a strongly incriminating evaluation implying willful and corrupt disobedience of the commandments of God. At the conclusion of His series of denouncements, Jesus Christ closed His address with the question, "How can ye escape the damnation (*krisis*) of *Gehenna*?" With these words He warns of the most ultimate judgment, again using Hinnom to represent the destruction of body and soul. His Jewish audience most surely made the fiery connection on all such occasions, calling to mind the familiar prophesies below:

> Thine hand shall find out all Thine enemies: Thy right hand shall find out those that hate Thee. Thou shalt make them as a fiery oven in the time of Thine anger: The Lord shall swallow

them up in His wrath, and the fire shall *devour* them. (Psalm 21:8-9)

For, behold, the day cometh, that shall burn as an oven; and all the proud, yea, and all that do wickedly, shall be stubble: and the day that cometh shall *burn them up*, saith the Lord of hosts, that it shall leave them neither root nor branch. (Malachi 4:1)

Completing the list of *Gehenna* occurrences is the aforementioned single use by the Apostle James. Gehenna is only mentioned in passing as he establishes the tongue as an uncontrollable evil which no man can bring into subjection. Nevertheless, we are reminded of the Lord's words about cutting off the offensive members that facilitate sin; notice how James makes a definite connection between a body part which acts as a stumblingblock, and the destructive fire which it deserves:

And the tongue is a fire, a world of iniquity: so is the tongue among our members, that it defileth the whole body, and setteth on fire the course of nature; and it is set on fire of hell ... But the tongue can no man tame; it is an unruly evil, full of deadly poison. Therewith bless we God, even the Father; and therewith curse we men, which are made after the similitude of God. (James 3:6,8-9)

Traditionally, *Gehenna* is usually defined as the final hell into which all of the wicked will enter for eternal conscious punishment. But, while *Gehenna* is certainly related to the unredeemed sinner, there is ample Biblical evidence to suggest that its fire will result in the destruction of such persons rather than their perpetual conscious torment. Having examined all twelve occurrences of the word, it must be conceded that none are able to provide us with a fully conclusive definition that confirms the traditional concept of "eternal hell." Instead we found the Lord speaking of the real fire of Hinnom, and using this fire symbolically to represent the actual fate of the unredeemed in the coming day of His wrath.

With this kind of symbolic speech, an interpretation is obviously called for, and the *KJV* translators made their own interpretation quite apparent when they rendered *Gehenna* as "hell," (and thereby gave us their explanation of the verses, rather than a true translation). But, in light of the many facts we have uncovered about man's mortality, an eternal hell is not necessarily the interpretation that is correct. If man is a mortal being who can only live forever through Jesus Christ, then it is logical to deduce that the Christless would be subject to only death and destruction when confronted with the judgment of *Gehenna*. There is sound reason to allow that this symbolic fire of God's judgment will "burn" the wicked until nothing but ashes remains.

Also symbolic of destruction is "the furnace of fire," an expression that is peculiar to the Gospel of Matthew, and occurs only two times in chapter 13. In explaining the parable of the tares, the Lord describes the end of the age when the unredeemed are gathered out and destroyed. Like the "goats" at the gathering of the nations (Matthew 25:31-46), these shall be executed, for they have no part in the new order that will subsequently begin:

> As therefore the tares are gathered and burned in the fire; so shall it be in the end of this world. The Son of Man shall send forth His angels, and they shall gather out of His kingdom all things that offend, and them which do iniquity; and shall cast them into a furnace of fire: there shall be wailing and gnashing of teeth. (Matthew 13:40-42)

The implication here is that the enemies of God shall be burned up, even as the tares are utterly destroyed in the flames. This solemn occasion will incite weeping and gnashing of teeth among the offending ones, but there is no statement to indicate that they will either burn or wail forever. As in the case of *Gehenna*, it is apparent that Jesus Christ used a symbolic figure here to invoke the visualization of a consuming judgment to come. Thus, the furnace of fire can be seen to represent the destruction of the unredeemed - not their consignment to "eternal hell." And like *Gehenna*, the furnace is given to emphasize the irreversible death of those who do not have the Son of God, and therefore, "hath not life" (1 John 5:12).

14. The fate of the unredeemed

While the godly man has laid hold on Jesus Christ - and therefore, life and immortality - the godless man must forever forfeit his life as the penalty for his transgressions. This forfeiture is characterized by an eternity of death within the grave, and in keeping, the Holy Spirit has used the strongest words in the Hebrew and Greek languages to teach us that the unsaved man is "perished" or "destroyed." We shall examine these words in more detail shortly, but let us first take a more general look at the fate of the unredeemed.

> When the wicked spring as the grass, and when all the workers of iniquity do flourish; it is that they shall be destroyed forever: but Thou, Lord, art most high for evermore. For, lo, Thine enemies, O Lord, for lo Thine enemies shall perish; all the workers of iniquity shall be scattered. (Psalm 92:7-9)

The psalmist tells us that the lawless shall "perish" and will be "destroyed forever," while the Lord is "most high for evermore." When taken literally and as written, this passage reveals that our God is eternal, whereas the wicked are not. Their "end" is again apparent in the next example, where the preserving of the righteous is set in contrast with the destruction of the unsaved.

> The Lord preserveth all them that love Him: but all the wicked will He destroy. (Psalm 145:20)

The message is simple here, and agrees with the basic concept of life for the godly man, and true death for the unsaved. Also of interest is yet another comparison, where the lasting nature of the man of God is set against the hopeless future of the unredeemed.

> Blessed is the man that walketh not in the counsel of the ungodly, nor standeth in the way of sinners, nor sitteth in the seat of the scornful. But his delight is in the law of the Lord; and in His law doth he meditate day and night. And he shall be like a tree planted by the rivers of water, that bringeth forth his fruit in his season; his leaf also shall not wither; and whatsoever he doeth shall prosper. The ungodly are not so: but are like the chaff which the wind driveth away. Therefore the ungodly shall not stand in the judgment, nor sinners in the congregation of the

righteous. For the Lord knoweth the way of the righteous; but the way of the ungodly shall perish. (Psalm 1)

The godly are likened to a tree that is planted by the rivers. Their leaf shall not wither - they shall have life - whereas the ungodly "are like the chaff which the wind driveth away." Chaff, the useless seed coverings of threshed grain, is discarded and decays leaving nothing. Therefore, (being as chaff), "the ungodly shall not stand in the judgment," for their "way" shall perish and resurrection shall be denied. When the Apostle Paul wrote of the unredeemed, he, too, speaks of a permanent destruction, thereby matching the concepts put forth in the Old Testament:

> And to you who are troubled rest with us, when the Lord Jesus shall be revealed from heaven with His mighty angels, in flaming fire, taking vengeance on them that know not God, and that obey not the gospel of our Lord Jesus Christ: who shall be punished with everlasting destruction from the presence of the Lord, and from the glory of His power. (2 Thessalonians 1:7-9)

When Jesus Christ reappears on the Earth, He will punish the uncovered sinner through "everlasting destruction." Here we see an execution which is final and irrevocable, as the Lord warned of when He spoke of *Gehenna*. Thus, "He will keep the feet of His saints, and the wicked shall be silent in darkness" (1 Samuel 2:9). Those who are destroyed forever will find an eternal dwelling in the depths of the grave.

> Drought and heat consume the snow waters: so doth the grave those which have sinned. The womb shall forget him; the worm shall feed sweetly on him; he shall be no more remembered; and wickedness shall be broken as a tree. (Job 24:19-20)

This is how God shall "break" wickedness; the evil man will be consumed within *sheol* and forgotten, rather than perpetuated in an eternal hell. The unsaved will sleep on forever – "no more remembered" – in a death which lasts for eternity. Note the Lord's use of the term "perpetual sleep" when He describes His destruction of the evil Babylonians:

> In their heat I will make their feasts, and I will make them drunken, that they may rejoice, and sleep a perpetual sleep, and not wake, saith the Lord. I will bring them down like lambs to the slaughter, like rams with he goats. (Jeremiah 51:39-40)

An air of finality is also evident in the following reference to the Rephaim, here translated as "deceased." Because of the Rephaim's peculiar nature (see 1 Peter 3:18-20, Appendix II), resurrection is denied to the entire group as a whole:

> They are dead, they shall not live; they are deceased, they shall not rise: therefore hast Thou visited and destroyed them, and made all their memory to perish. (Isaiah 26:14)

In the case of the Rephaim, there is no doubt but that they have all been forever destroyed in death. In the next example, we again see a portrayal of obliteration when the psalmist speaks of the Godless man:

> Thou hast rebuked the heathen, Thou hast destroyed the wicked, Thou hast put out their name for ever and ever. (Psalm 9:5)

The blotting out of names very much suggests that these persons have no future to speak of ... they will be "no more remembered," as Job said. Also implying non-existence for the unsaved are the words of Obadiah in the verse below. Here we read of the day of the Lord, and the fate that awaits the enemies of Israel:

> For as ye have drunk upon My holy mountain, so shall all the heathen drink continually, yea, they shall drink, and they shall swallow down, and they shall be as though they had not been. (Obadiah 16)

If the unsaved are to "be as though they had not been," then it is logical to conclude that nothing will remain of them.

> The wicked are overthrown and are not: but the house of the righteous shall stand. (Proverbs 12:7)

> For the evildoers shall be cut off: but those that wait upon the Lord, they shall inherit the earth. For yet a little while, and the wicked shall not be: Yea, thou shalt diligently consider his place, and it shall not be. But the meek shall inherit the earth; and shall delight themselves in the abundance of peace. (Psalms 37:9-11)

The contrast shows us that the godly will inherit the new world to come, but "the wicked shall not be." These words are very indicative of utter destruction, demonstrating again that the wages of sin is death, and nothing but. If the wicked are destined for eternal conscious torment, we wonder at how this could be totally ignored in a comparison which contrasts the future of the saved with that of the unsaved. We would expect to see the inheritance of a peaceful earth set against an eternal fate in hellfire; yet instead we are informed that the wicked have no existence and no "place." Instead of burning forever, Malachi 4:3 states that they "shall be ashes under the soles of your feet." Thus, the unsaved sinner inherits nothing at all, and we find instead that his life will be extinguished:

> For there shall be no reward to the evil man; the candle of the wicked shall be put out.
> (Proverbs 24:20)

Those who are judged worthy of everlasting destruction shall have their candle of life "put out" for all of eternity. The imagery of the proverb is brilliant here, for only the Lord can light a human candle, and in so doing, bestow life. Whereas there is no reward for the evil man, a recompense for the righteous is evident within our final verse. Death and destruction are sharply contrasted with the reward of life which is promised for those who love God's word.

> Whoso despiseth the word shall be destroyed: but he that feareth the commandment shall be rewarded. The law of the wise is a fountain of life, to depart from the snares of death.
> (Proverbs 13:13)

15. Perish/destroy/destruction: Hebrew words used to describe the penalty of sin.

When the Bible speaks of the unsaved man, we are most apt to read that he will be "perished," "lost," or "destroyed." Many have come to view these words as Divine euphemisms for an eternity of conscious torment, but there is no indication in the Scriptures themselves that we should so interpret. When the Lord told His disciples that "Our friend Lazarus sleepeth," and then, "Lazarus is dead," He made it quite clear that "sleep" is a God-given metaphor for death. There is no similar precedent in the Bible where (hypothetically) "Lazarus has perished" is followed by "Lazarus is lost to eternal conscious punishment in hell." And no writer in Scripture ever equates these two concepts in the plain language needed to establish that "perishing" was intended to convey a torturous eternal existence.

This being the case, there is good reason to believe that we are to take the key words regarding the fate of the unsaved at their literal meanings. "Perish" should be fully acknowledged as meaning just that, and "destruction" may likewise be accepted in its most primary sense. The word studies to follow, while by no means complete, will demonstrate how these words are ordinarily used in the Scriptures. Such an examination can bring valuable insight as to what the words mean when they are subsequently employed to describe the destiny of the unsaved.

First to be considered is the Hebrew *abad*, which is translated in the *KJV* as follows: "perish, be perished, be ready to perish, cause to perish, make to perish," (100 times); "destroy, be destroyed, destruction" (63 times); and, "be lost" (8 times), with one or two occurrences of "be broken," "be undone," "fail," "lose," and "spend." *Abad* is well defined by these translations, as the contexts of the following quotations will show.

> The field is wasted, the land mourneth; for the corn is wasted; the new wine is dried up, the oil languisheth. Be ye ashamed, O ye husbandmen; howl, O ye vinedressers, for the wheat and for the barley; because the harvest of the field is *perished*. (Joel 1:10-12)

Here we see *abad* used of a crop which is destroyed and fruitless. The vine is dried up and the corn is withered, leaving no harvest at all for the husbandmen to gather. The connotation is one of complete devastation and uselessness, as can also be seen in the passage below.

> Ye shall *utterly destroy* all the places, wherein the nations which ye shall possess served their gods, upon the high mountains, and upon the hills, and under every green tree: and ye shall overthrow their altars, and break their pillars, and burn their groves with fire; and ye shall hew down the graven images of their gods, and *destroy* the names of them out of that place. (Deuteronomy 12:2-3)

In ordering the Israelites to waste these idolatrous places, (literally, "destroying thou shalt destroy"), the Lord tells them to overthrow, break, burn, and hew down. *Abad* therefore implies a total ruin, with nothing remaining in a functional or usable condition. It is used by Eliphaz, below, to express the "end" of a living thing.

> The old lion *perisheth* for lack of prey, and the stout lion's whelps are scattered abroad. (Job 4:11)

Abad is the word used of an animal who starves to death, resulting in no more animal, and therefore, no more life. It is also used to describe the destruction of living people through death, as is evident in the words of the Israelites to Moses:

> "Behold, we die, we perish, *we* all *perish*. Whosoever cometh any thing near unto the tabernacle of the Lord shall die: shall we be consumed with dying?" (Numbers 17:12-13)

Thus, *abad* is used synonymously with dying. Those who "perish" die, or as in the case below, are killed by another.

> And when Athaliah the mother of Ahaziah saw that her son was dead, she arose and *destroyed* all the seed royal. But Johosheba, the daughter of king Joram, sister of Ahaziah, took Joash the son of Ahaziah, and stole him from among the king's sons which were slain. (2 Kings 11:1-2)

Athaliah "destroyed all the seed royal," and it is apparent that this involved the taking of their lives. In the next passage, we see again that destroying and killing people will cause them to "perish." In this instance we read of Haman's plot, by which he purposed to destroy all the Jews in Ahasuerus's kingdom:

> And the letters were sent by posts unto all the king's provinces, to destroy, to kill, *and to cause to perish*, all Jews, both young and old, little children and women, in one day. (Esther 3:13)

When used of living things, *abad* portrays death and dying. When employed to describe the fate of the unredeemed, its presence confirms that the penalty of sin is death:

> The Lord knoweth the days of the upright: and their inheritance shall be forever. They shall not be ashamed in the evil time: and in the days of famine they shall be satisfied. But the wicked shall *perish*, and the enemies of the Lord shall be as the fat of lambs: they shall consume; into smoke shall they consume away. (Psalm 37:18-20)

It is reasonable to concede that if *abad* means plain death and destruction in all the examples given, it may well mean plain death and destruction when used in reference to the expectation of the unredeemed. Thus, when David writes that "the wicked shall perish," he means that they shall die, be destroyed, and be no more. That an everlasting end is meant here can been seen by the comparison of futures ascribed to the opposing groups: the inheritance of the upright "shall be for ever," but "the wicked shall perish," and so, come to naught. Just as the harvest of the field (Joel 1:11) and the starving lion (Job 4:11), the Godless shall consume away into nothingness. The figures of fire and burning are again used to depict utter destruction; the end of the wicked is likened to the melting fat of the sacrificial lamb, and they shall dissipate into nothing, even as its smoke.

> Let God arise, let His enemies be scattered: let them also that hate Him flee before Him. As smoke is driven away, so drive them away: as wax melteth before the fire, so let the wicked *perish* at the presence of God. (Psalm 68:1-2)

In this final example of *abad*, another simile is used which helps to demonstrate the meaning of the word. The wicked are poetically observed as fleeing away from the Lord, and as being driven away as smoke. When coming near to His presence, their perishing is likened to melting wax, which burns away completely and leaves not a trace. This figure is quite suggestive of complete death and utter destruction. In fact, the Bible's melting wax and burning fat are essentially antagonistic to the traditional view of the eternal sinner; for while the more popular view portrays the wicked as remaining forever indestructible within the flames of hell, the Scriptural figures indicate that they will actually succumb to the fire of God.

The Hebrew *shamad* is also pertinent here, and has been translated in the *KJV* in the following manner: "destroy, be destroyed" (85 times), "utterly" (2 times), and once each by "destruction," "be overthrown," "perish," "bring to naught," and "pluck down." Usage shows that *shamad* can mean nothing other than "destroy," and it has been translated as such in 86 of its 92 occurrences.

> And Jacob said to Simeon and Levi, "Ye have troubled me to make me to stink among the inhabitants of the land, among the Canaanites and the Perizzites: and I being few in number, they shall gather themselves together against me, and slay me; and I *shall be destroyed*, I and my house." (Genesis 34:30)

Here Jacob indicates that *shamad* is synonymous with death; if Jacob is slain, he shall be "destroyed." Loss of life is also evident in the next quotation, where the people of Israel engage in battle:

> And all the spoil of these cities, and the cattle, the children of Israel took for a prey unto themselves; but every man they smote with the edge of the sword, until *they had destroyed them*, neither left they any to breathe. (Joshua 11:14)

Shamad is used to describe the death of the enemies of Israel, and in a way that leaves little doubt as to what this word means. Another example has Moses addressing the People themselves, and again it is death which is obviously indicated.

> And ye murmured in your tents, and said, 'Because the Lord hated us, He hath brought us forth out of the land of Egypt, to deliver us into the hand of the Amorites, to *destroy* us.' (Deuteronomy 1:27)

The people of Israel feared mortal injury at the hand of their enemies; to be *shamad*, is to be killed ... to be put to the utter destruction which occurs at death. When *shamad* is used to compare the future of the wicked with that of the redeemed, its blunt destruction is set against the eternal portion of the people of God:

The Lord knoweth the days of the upright: and their inheritance shall be for ever ... Mark the perfect man, and behold the upright: for the end of that man is peace. But the transgressors *shall be destroyed* together: the end of the wicked shall be cut off. (Psalm 37:18,37-38)

Thus, like *abad*, *shamad* may also be seen to describe death when used in reference to the fate of the wicked. The upright shall live in peace "for ever," but the lawless, in contrast, "shall be destroyed." Note that David additionally states here that the wicked shall be "cut off," or *kahrath*; when used of Jesus Christ in a prophecy of the Messiah (Daniel 9:26), this word undoubtedly referred to His death, and nothing more.

Shamad is also utilized in Psalm 145:20, where we have read, "The Lord preserveth all them that love Him: but all the wicked will He *destroy*." The traditional view is that *all* men are preserved - some for an eternity of bliss, and others for an eternity of suffering. But the forthright language of the Old Testament fully allows that the penalty of sin is only death within the grave. *Abad* and *shamad* both denote total and complete destruction, and therefore may be properly used to describe the Adamic death of us all. When a man has no saviour who can redeem him from this death, then the condition remains permanent, and the wages of sin are paid out eternally.

16. Perish/destroy/lose: Greek words used to describe the penalty of sin.

In the New Testament, as the Messiah enters, there is a continuation of the teaching which contrasts eternal life with death. Jesus Christ comes into the world offering life through His name, but in that offering it was sadly inevitable that many would refuse in unbelief - many would be "lost," be "destroyed," and "perish." When we examine the key Greek words to discover how they are typically employed, we shall find that they, too, describe death and destruction. When used in the context of man's eternal expectations, they are the dismal opposite of everlasting life.

Our first word, *apollumi*, is translated in the *KJV* as "perish" (33 times), "destroy" (23 times), "lose" (21 times), "be destroyed" (3 times), "be lost" (10 times), "be marred" (once), and "die" (once). A brief exploration of some of the occurrences of *apollumi* will yield its definition by contrast and context.

> No man putteth new wine into old bottles; else the new wine will burst the bottles, and be spilled, and the bottles shall *perish*. But new wine must be put into new bottles; and both are preserved. (Luke 5:37-38)

In this first example, we see the Lord use a pointed contrast between *apollumi* and preservation. While the use of old bottles may cause the ruin of both wine and containers, the use of new bottles will assure the useful preservation of both. *Apollumi* describes that which is made useless or spoiled.

> And if thy right hand offend thee, cut it off, and cast it from thee: for it is profitable for thee that one of thy members should *perish*, and not that thy whole body should be cast into hell. (Matthew 5:29-30)

Here *apollumi* is used by the Lord to describe the fate of a dismembered body part. A hand that is removed from the body will obviously decay and be no more. It shall corrupt throughout, and is used as a sober warning of what will happen to the entire body if a person is judged worthy of *Gehenna's* destruction. Thus, *apollumi* is used of something that is brought to nought, or something that comes to a final end. When the Lord tells his disciples of the sudden coming of the flood, He uses *apollumi* to describe the ending of human lives:

> They did eat, they drank, they married wives, they were given in marriage, until the day that Noe entered the ark, and the flood came, and *destroyed* them all. (Luke 17:27)

Like the Hebrew *abad* and *shamad, apollumi* is used to represent the destruction that occurs at death. Note the words of the Lord's disciples when they are shipboard with Him during the tempest at sea:

> And His disciples came to Him and awoke Him, saying, "Lord, save us: *we perish.*" (Matthew 8:25)

Here the disciples feared the loss of their lives, so that the "perishing" of *apollumi* is seen to be indicative of death. Note the sharp contrast in the verse to follow, where the saving or preserving of life is set against the simple destruction of it.

> Then said Jesus unto them, "I will ask you one thing; Is it lawful on the sabbath days to do good, or to do evil? to save life, or *to destroy* it?" (Luke 6:9)

As "good" is the opposite of "evil" in this example, so also is *apollumi* the opposite of "saving." Life is either preserved or destroyed ... saved or lost. When the Lord makes another comparison in the Gospel of John, the loss of life implied by *apollumi* is again very clear:

> The thief cometh not, but for to steal, and to kill, and to *destroy*: I am come that they might have life, and that they might have it more abundantly. (John 10:10)

The thief who takes life is contrasted with the One Who can give it back; thus, plain death and destruction are set against the abundant eternal life that is available through Jesus Christ. *Apollumi* - and the plain death that it represents - is shown to be an opposite of everlasting life, and it is used in just such a manner in this next familiar passage from John:

> And as Moses lifted up the serpent in the wilderness, even so must the Son of man be lifted up: that whosoever believeth in

Him *should* not *perish*, but have eternal life. For God so loved the world, that He gave His only begotten Son, that whosoever believeth in Him *should* not *perish*, but have everlasting life. (John 3:14-16)

When we see *apollumi* used in this obvious contrast with eternal life, it is not difficult to allow that simple death and destruction is the intended meaning of "perish." "Spiritual death" in hell is often interpreted as the true reality here, but neither the term nor the doctrine is spelled out within the Scriptures. We have seen prior evidence that man does not live eternally by nature, but that he must obtain a covering for sin in order to be justified to life. Being without the saving faith that is required, the unredeemed shall perish through death - shall consume away into nothing as the burning fat of a lamb (Psalm 37:20). So shall the wicked "be destroyed forever" (Psalm 92:7), but the righteously faithful will never be lost:

My sheep hear My voice, and I know them, and they follow Me: and I give unto them eternal life; and they *shall* never *perish*, neither shall any man pluck them out of My hand. (John 10:27-28)

Although the Lord's sheep may suffer Adamic death, their lives are hid with Christ in God, and no man can threaten their inheritance. The promise of resurrection and life assures that the faithful shall "never perish," whereas the promise of death and destruction assures that the wicked certainly will.

A secondary (but very relevant) meaning of *apollumi* describes the utter loss that is suffered in a solemn situation. In the example that follows, again from the Gospel of John, the Lord makes reference to the loaves that were multiplied.

When they were filled, He said unto His disciples, "Gather up the fragments that remain, that nothing *be lost*." (John 6:12)

Here *apollumi* is used to warn against the loss of that which could not be expected to be regained. When this secondary sense of *apollumi* is used in regard to a living being, death may be implied as in the Lord's words below.

> And bring hither the fatted calf, and kill it; and let us eat, and be merry: for this my son was dead, and is alive again; he was *lost*, and is found. (Luke 15:23-24)

The son who was assumed to be dead was referred to as "lost," since his life was as good as gone to the father who loved him. In the next verse the Lord is again using *apollumi*, this time to express the eternal security of His faithful.

> And this is the Father's will Which hath sent Me, that of all which He hath given me I should *lose nothing*, but should raise it up again at the last day. (John 6:39)

Those who are in Christ shall not be utterly lost to death and destruction, but shall live once again through His power of resurrection. The unredeemed, however, are "lost" for as long as they remain in sin's grasp, and *apollumi* is used to describe their unfortunate condition:

> But if our gospel be hid, it is hid to them *that are lost*: in whom the god of this world hath blinded the minds of them which believe not, lest the light of the glorious gospel of Christ ... should shine unto them. (2 Corinthians 4:3-4)

Thus, "the lost" are those who are without the light of the gospel, and *apollumi* represents both their current and future dilemmas. Those who are lost in this world are "perishing" even now and are "abiding in death" (1 John 3:14), for sin is continually working toward that one inescapable end. When this secondary meaning of *apollumi* is used in reference to the question of man's eternal future, we can see that it may very well describe that irretrievable loss of life which must inevitably occur among the unbelieving - and, therefore, it does not necessarily represent a loss to eternal hell. Lives and persons shall be lost and destroyed forever, surrendering to death with no hope of being "found."

The last word to receive our attention is the Greek *apoleia*, which is a noun derived from *apollumi*. It occurs only twenty times in the New Testament, where it is variously translated in the *KJV* as "perdition" (8 times), "destruction" (5 times), "waste" (2 times), "die" (once), "pernicious ways" (once), "damnation" (once), "damnable" (once), and "perish" (once). Examination of its usage will show that like *apollumi*, *apoleia* is also used of man's death, and it is also contrasted with the eternal life promised through Jesus Christ. A few examples are given below, where the loss of life is always apparent.

'It is not the manner of the Romans to deliver any man to *die*, before that he which is accused have the accusers face to face, and have licence to answer for himself concerning the crime laid against him.' (Acts 25:16)

In this verse, *apoleia* refers to death by execution, and it is used by Festus in declaring "Paul's cause" (verse 14) before King Agrippa. Since *apoleia* is used to describe plain and simple death here, there is nothing to preclude its meaning "death" in the Gospel of Matthew, as well:

> Enter ye in at the strait gate: for wide is the gate, and broad is the way, that leadeth to *destruction*, and many there be which go in thereat: because strait is the gate, and narrow is the way, which leadeth unto life, and few there be that find it. (Matthew 7:13-14)

"The way that leadeth to destruction" is contrasted with the narrow way that leads unto life. Taken literally and as written, we again see that death is the expectation of the unfaithful. When Paul later speaks of the backsliding Christian, he maintains that *apoleia* is the fate towards which the weakening will slide.

> Now the just shall live by faith: but if any man draw back, My soul shall have no pleasure in him. But we are not of them who draw back unto *perdition*; but of them that believe to the saving of the soul. (Hebrews 10:38-39)

Those who "draw back unto perdition"[4] are turning away from their faith and sliding back towards death and destruction. Paul encourages the Jews to be of "them that believe to the saving of the *psuche*," and thereby contrasts *apoleia* with the saving of the life.

In conclusion, we see that *apollumi, apoleia, abad,* and *shamad,* are synonymous with our English "destroy," "destruction," and "perish." All of these words have been demonstrated to convey death or complete loss of man or object. Therefore, when reading that the unsaved of humanity will "perish," it is not illogical to conclude that they will suffer destruction through death, rather than torment in eternal hellfire.

---

[4] The archaic definition of "perdition" is that of "utter destruction," and as the *KJV* utilizes archaic English, this is the meaning that should be adhered to here.

The wages of sin is said to be "death," and where there is no covering for sin, a state of extinction must reign on perpetually as a just and everlasting punishment. Whereas the godly will be "preserved" to inherit for eternity, the wicked "shall be destroyed for ever" with no possibility of redemption from the grave (Psalm 145:20, Psalm 92:7).

It is evident that the writers of Scripture have expressed the fate of the unredeemed in plain and simple words, and there is no directive for us to interpret these as "spiritual death," "eternal separation from God," or "eternal conscious punishment in hell." When the words are understood in their primary senses, and are freed from any additional meanings which have been attached by men, the fate of the unredeemed is seen to be in full agreement with other Bible teachings on the nature of death, the soul, the emptiness of *sheol*, and the destructive power of *Gehenna*.

17. The lake of fire and the second death

Last to be considered is the Bible's final fire of judgment - the formidable lake which burns with brimstone. It is mentioned only five times in the Scriptures, and these occurrences are all to be found in the book of Revelation. Since this book is abundant with symbolic and cryptic prophecy concerning the end-time, we should not be unwilling to entertain the possibility that the lake, too, is a mere symbol given to represent a reality. The Lord's use of *Gehenna* has shown us that He is quite willing to use figures in this manner, even to describe the destiny of those who do not have the justification to life. But regardless of whether the lake of fire is literal or symbolic, it has a very significant role to play at the end-time which will accomplish God's goal of putting an end to sin and death.

Because Revelation is a book rich with symbolic representations, extreme care must be taken when attempting to gather hard facts within its pages. In many instances, the best we can do is to propose educated guesses based on what we know from other portions of the Scriptures. If the vision seems to be stating a contradiction to what is clearly taught elsewhere, then it is most likely that the student is facing an allegorical symbol or a figure of speech. In our particular area of study, the most relevant truths that we should take into Revelation from other areas of the Bible are these: that man is born a totally mortal being, that his attainment of eternal existence is only by faith, and that the fate of the faithless – the unredeemed – is an everlasting destruction. These concepts are strongly supported by multiple non-visionary writings that we have seen thus far and it would be unfortunate if we were tempted to forsake them in order to allow a fully traditional interpretation of the fiery lake - i.e., the lake as being an eternal hell of conscious agony. With these thoughts in mind, let us now consider the lake of fire/second death within its context of the end-time. The quotation given here is a lengthy one, but is necessary to establish the sequence of the events shown to John within his vision. As we begin reading, the tribulation has climaxed and the Lord is about to return to the Earth.

And I saw heaven opened, and behold, a white horse; and He that sat upon him was called Faithful and True, and in righteousness He doth judge and make war ... And I saw the beast, and the kings of the earth, and their armies, gathered together to make war against Him That sat on the horse, and against His army. And the beast was taken, and with him the false prophet that wrought miracles before him, with which he deceived them that had received the mark of the beast, and them that worshipped his image. These both were cast alive into a *lake of fire* burning with brimstone. And the remnant were slain with the sword of Him That sat upon the horse, which sword proceeded out of His mouth: and all the fowls were filled with their flesh. And I saw an angel come down from heaven, having the key of the bottomless pit and a great chain in his hand. And he laid hold on the dragon, that old serpent, which is the Devil, and Satan, and bound him a thousand years, and cast him into the bottomless pit, and shut him up, and set a seal upon him, that he should deceive the nations no more, till the thousand years should be fulfilled: and after that he must be loosed a little season. And I saw thrones, and they sat upon them, and judgment was given unto them; and I saw the souls of them that were beheaded for the witness of Jesus, and for the word of God, and which had not worshipped the beast, neither his image, neither had received his mark upon their foreheads, or in their hands; and they lived and reigned with Christ a thousand years. But the rest of the dead lived not again until the thousand years were finished. This is the first resurrection. Blessed and holy is he that hath part in the first resurrection: on such the *second death* hath no power, but they shall be priests of God and of Christ, and shall reign with Him a thousand years.

And when the thousand years are expired, Satan shall be loosed out of his prison, and shall go out to deceive the nations which are in the four quarters of the earth, Gog and Magog, to gather them together to battle: the number of whom is as the sand of the sea. And they went up on the breadth of the earth, and compassed the camp of the saints about, and the beloved city: and fire came down from God out of heaven, and devoured them. And the devil that deceived them was cast into the *lake of fire* and brimstone, where the beast and the false prophet are, and shall be tormented day and night for ever and ever. And I saw a great white throne, and Him that sat on it, from Whose face the earth and the heaven fled away; and there was found no place for them. And I saw the dead, small and great, stand before God; and the books were opened: and another book was opened, which is the book of life: and the dead were judged out of those things which were written in the books, according to their works. And the sea gave up the dead which were in it; and death and hell delivered up the dead which were in them: and they were judged every man according to their works. And death and hell were cast into the *lake of fire*. This is *the second death*. And whosoever was not found written in the book of life was cast into the *lake of fire*.

And I saw a new heaven and a new earth; for the first heaven and the first earth were passed away. (Revelation 19:11, 19:19-21:1)

According to John's vision, the beast and the false prophet are the first to be cast into the "lake of fire burning with brimstone." After the thousand year reign of Christ and the rebellion of the nations, Satan is also cast in, followed by Death, *Hades*, and those of the second resurrection whose names are not written in the book of life.

Now Ezekiel 28:11-19 indicates that Satan's end is destruction by fire, and that he will be brought to ashes upon the earth for all to see. We also know for certain that death will be destroyed (1 Corinthians 15:26), and that *sheol*/*hades*/death will likewise come to naught (Hosea 13:14). Thus, when we see John revealing that he saw all three of these evils cast into the lake of fire, we have good reason to consider the lake as an instrument of destruction or termination, rather than one of eternal conscious torment ..... for obviously, these things are going to come to a conclusion here, they are not going to continue on. It would not be a stretch of the imagination then to assume that the beast and the false prophet will meet their end in the lake as well. But with such a proposal, Revelation 20:10 may be troubling to some:

> "The devil that deceived them was cast into the lake of fire and brimstone, *where the beast and the false prophet are*, and shall be tormented day and night *for ever and ever*." (Revelation 20:10)

Since the beast and the false prophet will be cast into the lake one thousand years prior to Satan, we may well wonder why this verse seems to indicate that they are still alive in there when Satan is cast in. The difficulty is only a matter of the translation, however, for the word "are" has been added where there is no corresponding word in the Greek text. The purpose of the clause is to ascertain that this is the self-same lake that the beast and the false prophet entered, and it is therefore quite reasonable that it should be read, "where the beast and the false prophet were," or for more clarity, "were cast." (Or, as the *NIV* has it, "had been thrown.)

There is also a legitimate concern about the stated time period of Satan's "torment" in 20:10, a torment which must, naturally, precede his destruction. This is said to go on "day and night for ever and ever," and some translations, such as the *NIV,* include the beast and the false prophet in this torment: *"They"* will be tormented day and night for ever and ever." In the case of Satan, of whom we have additional information, this seemingly contradicts Isaiah 14:12-15 and the account in Ezekiel 28, which states, "never shalt thou be anymore." However, since the Ezekiel account gives us a clear impression of Satan's destruction, it should be given careful consideration in light of the highly symbolic imagery of the Revelation. John has given us a prophecy which is deliberately obscure and mysterious, and which is presented in a very artful and dramatic fashion. In 20:8, for instance, we are told that the armies of Gog and Magog will number "as the sand of the sea." This particular kind of statement is quite similar to the torment that continues "for ever and ever," for both verses are examples of hyperbole: a figure of speech in which excessive exaggeration is employed to make a stronger impression upon the reader. While the armies that will compass the camp of the saints will most certainly be immense, it is very doubtful that we are intended to take the number of "the sand" literally. Likewise, the destruction of Satan will be preceded by a very great "torment" that will be very enduring, and probably also very unpleasant. But the words of Ezekiel confirm that a figure of speech is being used here for emphasis; although his torment may be prolonged, Satan himself shall most certainly die. (For pertinent information on the word "torment," see notes on *basanidzo* under Revelation 14:9-11, Appendix II.)

After the beast, the false prophet, and the great antagonist meet with their doom in the lake, John's vision indicates that the second resurrection and its judgment will take place. But before discussing the lake as it pertains to this particular group of people, it will be beneficial to observe the remaining Biblical mentions of both the lake of fire and the second death. The fifth and last occurrence of the lake appears in Revelation 21:8, where Jesus Christ is speaking to John. His words are more particular about the nature of those who will be subjected to the fire, and notably, He contrasts these people with those who will "inherit all things."

> He that overcometh shall inherit all things; and I will be his God, and he shall be my son. But the fearful, and unbelieving, and the abominable, and murderers, and whoremongers, and sorcerers, and idolaters, and all liars, shall have their part in *the lake which burneth with fire* and brimstone: which is *the second death*. (Revelation 21:7-8)

Although it would appear that "the second death" is another name for the lake of fire itself, the expression is also very likely to pertain to the action of being "cast in." "The second death" occurs just four times in the Bible, and like the lake of fire, it, too, appears exclusively in Revelation. We have already seen three of those occurrences in the quotations above, and the last, which occurs much earlier in Revelation, is as follows:

> Fear none of those things which thou shalt suffer: behold, the devil shall cast some of you into prison, that ye may be tried; and ye shall have tribulation ten days: be thou faithful unto death, and I will give thee a crown of life. He that hath an ear, let him hear what the Spirit saith unto the churches; He that overcometh shall not be hurt of *the second death*. (Revelation 2:10-11)

It is the Lord's promise that those who are "faithful unto death" during the end-time trouble will be given the reward of a crown of life. Such people will certainly be some of the great martyrs and champions of the faith, and they will be held in such high esteem that they "shall not be hurt of the second death." These overcomers are obviously included within the first resurrection of Revelation 20 - "them that were beheaded for the wit-ness of Jesus, and for the word of God" - and it is there reaffirmed that "the second death hath no power" over the entire group. (20:6). Thus, many who are raised to life in the first resurrection will apparently carry with them a mark of distinction brought about by their superior acts of faith. In addition to an exemption from the lake of fire, their reward is to reign with Christ in His kingdom for a thousand years before the "rest of the dead" are quickened.

As to the second resurrection, John's vision implies that it will be a more massive one in which the sea, Death, and *Hades* deliver up the dead which are in them. After the works of these people have been judged out of "the books," Death (who rode the horse) and *Hades* (who followed after him) are cast into the lake of fire, (and as discussed previously, this action clearly represents the end of dying and the state of death). Then an unknown percentage of those people who came before the throne for judgment enter the lake, as well: those whose names do not appear in the book of life. Traditionally, this part of the vision is interpreted as the entrance of the wicked into eternal hell, where their perpetually living souls will be separated from God and imprisoned in flames for eternity.

But, as we have seen repeatedly in the pages leading up to this chapter, the Scriptures have said that the wages of sin is death, and that the fate of the wicked is to be destroyed forever. "Soul" has been demonstrated to be mortal no matter how it is used in the Bible, and the "spirit" in man and the animals has been shown to be the property of God Himself. And so death, when it happens, is not a conscious state of activity for an eternally living soul, but rather, a state of utter destruction which has been metaphorically compared to the unconscious state of "sleep." In light of these things, it seems very unlikely that God has constructed an eternal hell of torment for eternal unredeemed people, for their destiny is the emptiness of death with a total absence of life. And so, accordingly, when looking at the lake of fire and the second death, it is simply inappropriate to envision an eternal life of everburning torment for those who, without salvation, must surely perish in order that sin may perish too. All the Scripture has said thus far would indicate that destruction, not hell, is what the lake of fire is all about.

Finally, the context in which the second death appears suggests that it denotes a complete "wrap up" of the world which is now. As God takes care of His earth-related business in Revelation 20, He effectively brings an end to sin and death through the person of Jesus Christ. After those who have been covered by the blood of the Lamb are redeemed from death in victorious resurrection, death, and the grave are destroyed forever, with their end implying man's irrevocable eternal life. As far as the unsaved are concerned, there is nothing for God to do towards them except to continue to pay them the wages of sin ... for their lack of faith has brought them an eternally enduring death. Thus while "the law of sin and death" remains forever in force for the unredeemed, "the law of the Spirit of life in Christ" assures eternal life for the people of God (Romans 8:2).

In John's vision, the new heaven and new earth appear directly after the fiery judgment events, and we enter into a new world where there will be "no more death, neither sorrow, nor crying, neither shall there be any more pain: for the former things are passed away" (Revelation 21:4). Traditionally, these blessings are interpreted to pertain only to the redeemed, while the eternal wicked continue to suffer endlessly in a hell of perpetual torments. But consider that these words are true without exception: that there will be no more death, sorrow, crying or pain anywhere, at anytime ... not in the new heavens and earth, and not in an eternal hell of fire. In such a case, the former things *would* be passed away, bringing a complete end to sin and sinners, and leaving only perfection in God's new world to come.

20. Concluding comments

Immortality of the soul is by far the most popular and well known doctrine concerning the nature of man, but it is not the only conclusion that one may arrive at through the study of the Bible. Another result has been demonstrated in previous pages and it is acceptably sound in that it is in accordance with the Scriptures. Many have considered its point of view to be meritorious because it gives a fuller answer to the problem of sin and death while granting larger meaning to the issues of salvation and resurrection. With the exception of symbolic, figurative, and visionary works - which rightfully require careful *interpretation* - a straightforward reading of the Bible will justify the conclusion that man is not inherently immortal or eternal, and that the penalty of sin is to remain dead forever. But, by the grace of God, we have seen that each man has the opportunity to choose between an eternity within the grave, or an everlasting existence. Life is lost to all through the Adamic condemnation, but is able to be gained again through the person of Jesus Christ. In addition to the Scriptural evidence already given for this plain death and resurrection viewpoint (i.e., conditional immortality), there are a few additional "arguments" which may also be of interest to the student. While these most likely have been encountered in the past, a re-examination may be useful as this study is brought to a close.

Firstly, it is generally agreed among Christians that the task of revealing the great doctrinal matters of the faith was given to the Apostle Paul. His magnificent writings contain the deeper truths which have enabled us to better comprehend our sinful nature, our need for redemption, and the righteousness we obtain through Jesus Christ. But in all of Paul's writings, there is no specific doctrine recorded regarding the alleged immortal nature of man's soul and spirit. The man wrote nothing of eternal conscious punishment, and gave no instruction concerning the traditional doctrine of "spiritual death."

If these things are indeed the truth, then it is curious that Paul missed so many opportunities to mention them. The apostle taught concisely concerning the first and second Adams in Romans, yet in addressing the principles of sin and death, he wrote nothing about the "spiritual death" of the unredeemed. He taught very plainly about "the wages of sin," but he never conveyed that the resulting death would consist of eternal hellfire and torment. And, while Paul also wrote a thorough treatment of resurrection in 1 Corinthians, he never mentioned the "eternal soul" or "eternal spirit," or that they would be joined with a newly raised body at the last trump. Was this man presenting an incomplete picture, or is it indeed possible that these things are not a part of the truth found in the Holy Scriptures? It would seem that the consistent beat of the apostle's drum is that death - just plain "death" as he states it - is the consequence of sin. If any New Testament writer could have been expected to broach such a doctrine as "spiritual death in hell," it would have been Paul and it would probably have appeared in Romans. If the orthodox view is in fact a true concept, then it is perplexing to find it altogether omitted from the foundational teaching on sin and death. Thus, the fact that Paul never addresses the subject at all leads one to question whether it is truly one of the elements comprising "all the counsel of God" (Acts 20:26).

Paul does make one single mention of *hades*, however, and this we have already seen in 1 Corinthians 15:55: "O death, where is thy sting? O *grave* where is thy victory?" And so, the apostle employs his single use of *hades* to describe not a spiritual dwelling place for "eternal souls," but resurrection's great triumph over death and the grave. Throughout his writings in the New Testament Scriptures, Paul remained utterly silent on the subject of hell as it is known today. He mentions death often, and it has become traditional for many of these mentions to be interpreted as "spiritual death," or eternal separation from God within hell. But an explicit pronouncement of everlasting conscious torment as the penalty for man's sin, has not been recorded by Paul, or any other writer of Scripture. Everlasting *fire* does not necessarily imply the everlasting conscious existence of those who are subjected to it.

Also of interest is the question of sin's longevity: whether it is to be a destroyed enemy, or an eternal fixture that will endure forever. It is evident that one of God's great purposes throughout the Bible is the removal of sin from mankind in order to achieve perfection in the world to come. But this is something that could not be fully realized if sin were allowed to perpetuate for all of eternity within a hell of conscious torment. For how could God ever be "all in all," and how could it be said that "the former things are passed away," if sin, sinners, and even Satan, yet remain? Sin is the root cause of death, corruption, and all evil; the suggestion that God will preserve another world of sin and "spiritually dead" sinners in a separate location just doesn't seem to be a complete solution to the problem of sin. Evil would be contained in such a circumstance, but it would never come to an end, and it would be entitled to claim "victory" over all that it received unto itself. It could even be argued that evil might "win" the majority of mankind, and that the eternal hell would remain a perpetual monument to the fact that God did not fully prevail over sin.

But we have assurance that death will be destroyed, and it seems logical to expect that sin, its intimate partner, will likewise have no part to play in the new heavens or the new earth. This assumption is ably supported by that unspeakable thought left unexpressed in Genesis 3:22. If God had allowed man to continue partaking of the tree of life in his fallen state, man would have truly become an unstoppable immortal sinner. "So He drove out the man" and put the tree under the guard of the Cherubims (verse 24) until the problem of sin could be fully resolved through Jesus Christ.

Those who believe in the inherent immortality of man often cite the popular premise that sin, as a condition, is everlasting within the "eternal soul" of the unredeemed. It is frequently taught that it is the soul of a man that is infected with Adamic sin; and thus, when an unsaved man loses his physical life, his sin-laden soul is said to pass into eternity, forever in the fallen state known as "spiritual death." But the Scriptures teach that it is man's *body* that is afflicted with the curse of sin, not an eternal entity. Paul informs us in Romans that "the law of sin" is contained within our "members" (Romans 7:23), and since it is the body that is afflicted, it naturally follows that it is the body which actually dies because of sin. This is in full harmony with the fundamental point that has been discussed in chapter 2 and throughout the length of this study; namely, that the penalty of sin is a total return to the dust, and not a figurative death of the "eternal spirit," as is often proposed.

According to Paul, it is "the flesh" that serves the law of sin (Romans 7:25), and it is likewise the flesh of man that is declared to be sinful (Romans 8:3). Thus, we see Paul encouraging the Romans to "let not sin ... reign in your mortal body" (Romans 6:12), for indeed the body - and it's natural mind - is the only possible human medium in which sin can reign. In suit, when a man's body of flesh is destroyed through death, he is then no longer under sin's dominion, for "he that is dead is freed from sin" (Romans 6:7). Sin no longer prevails over the man who has died, for a dead man has no being, and has therefore no capability for evil thought, intent, or action. It is for this very reason that God "reckons" that the redeemed Christian's "*body* is dead because of sin" (Romans 8:10) - so that He might regard His people to be dead to the sin which inherently resides within them as long as they are living. Death brings with it a release from sin's bond, and when we are "reckoned" to be dead, then we are also reckoned to be free from sin (Romans 6:6,7,11,22).

But Paul's doctrine is made of little effect if we allow that sin can follow a man into death via "the eternal soul," (In that case, it would follow and defile the redeemed man as well as the unredeemed.) Thus, we see a definite time stated within the Scriptures when sin no longer dominates a man; it comes to an end in each individual person, and that end occurs when the body of sin is destroyed. "Sin, when it is finished, bringeth forth death" (James 1:15), and when death is upon a man, sin has completed its course within him. We can see, therefore, a certain logic in the complete destruction that is suffered at death, for the body (and its flawed mind of flesh) must be destroyed in order that its sin will not prevail. Resurrection will then be employed to restore and rebuild the redeemed, that each personality might be quickened with a pure and spiritual body which is fashioned like that of the risen Lord's.

Following this train of thought, it can be seen that the Bible's doctrine of death and resurrection allows that God will fully accomplish the removal of sin from His creation. With the law of sin residing in man's mortal flesh, (rather than in an "eternal soul"), all men are naturally released from sin upon their death. Those who are unbelieving shall "not see life," and so they, and their sin, will come to an end via the penalty of everlasting destruction. And while the saints shall rise and live for eternity, they shall be quickened to life without the undesirable and fatal flaw. The final curtain will ring down on sin after the return of Christ and the end of the millennium to follow. Once the lake of fire has completely devoured the root of sin and its evil works, the heavens and earth shall be wonderfully recreated, and there will be no trace remaining of the corruption which sin brought to man and his environment.

The next point to be considered is a basic one, which strikes at the very foundation of the principle of redemption. If we believe that the penalty of sin is not simply natural death, but "spiritual death," then it should follow that Christ would have to die "spiritually" in order to pay that penalty for us. This is only reasonable, and would mean that Jesus Christ should suffer eternal conscious punishment in hell - and eternal separation from the Father - if He were to actually be our substitute, and thus save us from such a fate. Yet we know from the Scriptures that this has not been the case; His suffering for our sin is over now, and Christ presently sits at the right hand of God the Father. This produces a disturbing inequality within the traditional doctrine, provoking us to ask whether the penalty of sin is the same for both the sinner and the Saviour Who claims to have paid the penalty in his place. For when Jesus Christ died for man's sins, He suffered only a six hour death on the cross ... but, when man dies for his own sins, the traditional view is that he must suffer an eternity of torment in hell. The orthodox doctrine seems unbalanced, having our Lord make an incomplete payment for our sin: the blood of His flesh has been spilled, but the spiritual penalty of hell is left unaddressed. Thus, the traditional view presents Jesus Christ as man's substitute, yet He does not actually experience the eternal consequences that man is believed to merit himself.

But, if the penalty of sin is death - simple, natural death, and nothing else - then by every account the Saviour has made payment in full. The Bible gives numerous references to Christ's death on the cross, and it is this death, with its spilled blood, that is proclaimed to have accomplished our atonement with God (Hebrews 9:15-22). Looked at in this light, the Saviour is truly our substitute in death, for He has died the very same death that man himself suffers due to his fallen condition. This wonderful substitution means that the Christian's death is no longer viewed by God as his or her payment for sin. Another Man forfeited His life for us, and our own death then became a mere necessary evil - a temporary "unclothed" state which shall be remedied in the proper season by resurrection. Since by "reckoning" we are already dead, already raised, and already alive unto God (Romans 6:3-11), our actual death should be of little significance to us. Our bodies of sinful flesh will pass away, as they must because they are sown in sin and corruption ... but because of the work of Jesus Christ, we shall be raised again in glory, never again to know sin or death.

When we acknowledge the important central position of death as both the consequence of man's sin and the Saviour's means of accomplishing atonement, we can then appreciate the rich significance of the lifeblood offerings of the law and of our Christ. Blood is highly significant when we link it to physical life and death, but seems quite irrelevant when we attempt to apply it to things spiritual. Thus, the mandatory shedding of blood as the requirement for remission of sin strongly implies that it is "physical death" that pays the penalty of sin, and not a "spiritual death." This is the penalty that the Saviour paid, and according to the plain words of Romans 6:23, it is also the one that mankind must pay.

Now let us turn to a final question, which is very often a root cause of skepticism regarding the Christian faith. If God's love for the world was such that He sacrificed His only Son for it, how consistent is it that He would eternally torment those who turn down His offer of salvation? Granted, some Christians may feel this to be a senseless question, pointing out that the Almighty righteousness of God requires that He punish sin in this enduring manner. But consider that this is often one of the very first questions asked by the potential or novice Christian, and for such a person the answer can be critical as to whether he advances into belief or not. For this reason it is a valid question, and one that must be answered convincingly.

To this author's mind, the most logical answer is a negative one; self-sacrificing love and endless revenge are not harmonious actions when attributed to a just and righteous God Who represents Himself as the loving Creator of all mankind. It is not consistent that the Father who gave His only Son, and Who delights in expressing His relationship to the world in terms of intimate family, would torturously punish His wayward and foolish creatures for all of eternity to come. Furthermore, because we know that our God is supremely righteous, we can trust His judgment of mankind to be absolutely fair. And, because He has revealed Himself as a merciful and compassionate God, we have good reason to believe that He may even be *more* than fair when it comes to the meting out of penalties and punishment

The traditional concept of eternal conscious punishment, however, gives us a scenario in which punishment does not seem to fit the crime, and the punisher is perceived as unjust and merciless. A lifetime of sin cannot be rightly punished with an eternity of miserable torment. When we add the consideration that every man since Adam has been born in a fallen state *through no fault of his own*, the injustice is vastly multiplied. Many people are able to recognize an unfairness and inconsistency here, and they will weigh these factors when making their decision for or against Christ. Many have turned away, and will continue to turn away, because they simply cannot reconcile "God is love" and "do good to them that hate you" with the hypocritical retribution of eternal conscious torment for those that hate Him, or simply ignore Him. Yes, the question of whether hell is "fair" or not is an important one for the potential Christian, and it is an important one for those who are established in the faith, as well. We are the ambassadors of God's word in the world today, and surely the Lord will hold us responsible for the way in which we represent Him to our listeners. Let every one search thoroughly for the truth about his God before he takes it upon himself to spread the word to others.

Some modern-day theologians are now teaching that the absolute holiness of God demands His everlasting wrath in the punishment for sin. It is often proclaimed that the wages of sin is an eternity in conscious torment, and that every man is destined for this fate unless he chooses Christ within his lifetime. Weighing the evidence for this position against the facts and arguments presented throughout this study, some Christians have chosen to depart from the mainstream teachings and embark upon a more lonely path in the desire to be found faithful to the truth. These agree that God is indeed absolutely holy, just, and righteous, but their understanding of the Scriptures leaves them unable to agree with the traditional doctrines of man's nature and the extreme price he must pay for inborn sin. For those who prefer a more straightforward approach to God's word, the views presented here can offer a sound alternative to the more popular interpretations of today's Christian leaders. This less popular view of God sees a Creator Who will pursue an active punishment of all evil within a *day* of wrath - not an eternity of wrath - and Who will preserve only those who love Him to live in everlasting peace.

In closing, we have seen that the doctrine of plain death and resurrection is a simple and uncomplicated one, leaving the matter-of-fact words of the Bible to speak for themselves. There is no need to add on additional concepts or to spiritualize in any way: life is life and death is death, just as it is written in the Book. The viewpoint does no damage to the word of God, neither does it disturb the Christian's hope of eternal life. Its only significant consequences are to recognize an interval of "sleep," and to omit the erroneous eternal conscious punishment of the lost. (A concept which came from the heart of man, rather than from the heart of God.) One must go without the assurance of living on continuously after death - and this may bother some readers - but what is the passage of time to those who are asleep? We shall pass from death to life with no awareness of the intervening years, "sleeping in Christ," and then awakening to glory. And lastly, with this view of the Bible, resurrection can truly be appreciated as the awe-inspiring miracle that it actually is. The Lord's great power is surely magnified when we marvel at His ability to quicken those who lie utterly dead within the grave.

God's intentions toward us are clear, for He wants His people to share with Him the joy of living together in communion for eternity. He loves the world that He has created and desires that we would all come to Him, and that none would be lost to death. But, unfortunately, there are many people who have no desire to know the Lord God. Some will deny His existence altogether, while others may suspect He is there, but do not feel the need to seek Him out. They never meditate upon His great deeds and the wonders of the universe, neither do they admire Him or respect Him in any way. These are the lost: their future is to perish forever - thoughtless, emotionless, sightless in the darkness - never to know God's wondrous glory and loving gifts.

Appendix 1: The Rich Man and Lazarus.

The story of The Rich Man and Lazarus is considered separately from the main text in order that it might be given special and detailed attention. Before opening discussion, a review of the passage will allow the student to become refamiliarized with the particulars and the sequence of events. The story is quoted within its full context, and thus appears as a part of the Lord's address to the Pharisees after His parable of The Unjust Steward. A fully conscious afterlife in *hades* is depicted, with torment for the selfish rich man, and comfort for the hungry beggar.

Luke 16:1-17:2

And He said also unto His disciples, "There was a certain rich man, which had a steward; and the same was accused unto him that he had wasted his goods. And he called him, and said unto him, 'How is it that I hear this of thee? give an account of thy stewardship; for thou mayest be no longer steward. Then the steward said within himself, 'What shall I do? for my lord taketh away from me the stewardship: I cannot dig; to beg I am ashamed. I am resolved what to do, that, when I am put out of the stewardship, they may receive me into their houses.' So he called every one of his lord's debtors unto him, and said unto the first, 'How much owest thou unto my lord?' And he said, 'An hundred measures of oil.' And he said unto him, 'Take thy bill, and sit down quickly, and write fifty.' Then said he to another, 'And how much owest thou?' And he said, 'An hundred measures of wheat.' And he said unto him, 'Take thy bill, and write fourscore.' And the lord commended the unjust steward, because he had done wisely: for the children of this world are in their generation wiser than the children of light. And I say unto you, 'Make to yourselves friends of the mammon of unrighteousness; that, when ye fail, they may receive you into everlasting habitations.' He that is faithful in that which is least is faithful also in much: and he that is unjust in the least is unjust also in much. If therefore ye have not been faithful in the unrighteous mammon, who will commit to your trust the true riches? And if ye have not been faithful in that which is another man's, who shall give you that which is your own? No servant can serve two masters; for either he will hate the one, and love the other; or else he will hold to the one, and despise the other. Ye cannot serve God and mammon."

And the Pharisees also, who were covetous, heard all these things: and they derided Him. And He said unto them, "Ye are they which justify yourselves before men; but God knoweth your hearts: for that which is highly esteemed among men is abomination in the sight of God. The law and the prophets were until John: since that time the kingdom of God is preached, and every man presseth into it. And it is easier for heaven and earth to pass, than one tittle of the law to fail. Whosoever putteth away his wife, and marrieth another, committeth adultery: and whosoever marrieth her that is put away from her husband committeth adultery.

There was a certain rich man, which was clothed in purple and fine linen, and fared sumptuously every day: and there was a certain beggar named Lazarus, which was laid at his gate, full of sores, and desiring to be fed with the crumbs which fell from the rich man's table: moreover the dogs came and licked his sores. And it came to pass, that the beggar died, and was carried by the angels into Abraham's bosom: the rich man also died, and was buried; and in hell (*hades*) he lift up his eyes, being in torments, and seeth Abraham afar off, and Lazarus in his bosom. And he cried and said, 'Father Abraham, have mercy on me, and send Lazarus, that he may dip the tip of his finger in water, and cool my tongue; for I am tormented in this flame.' But Abraham said, 'Son, remember that thou in thy lifetime receivedst thy good things, and likewise Lazarus evil things: but now he is comforted, and thou art tormented. And beside all this, between us and you there is a great gulf fixed: so that they which would pass from hence to you cannot; neither can they pass to us, that would come from thence.' Then he said, 'I pray thee therefore, father, that thou wouldest send him to my father's house: for I have five brethren; that he may testify unto them, lest they also come into this place of torment.' Abraham saith unto him, 'They have Moses and the prophets; let them hear them.' And he said, 'Nay, father Abraham: but if one went unto them from the dead, they will repent.' And he said unto him, 'If they hear not Moses and the prophets, neither will they be persuaded, though one rose from the dead.'"

Then said He unto the disciples, "It is impossible but that offences will come: but woe unto him, through whom they come! It were better for him that a millstone were hanged about his neck, and he cast into the sea, than that he should offend one of these little ones.

As it was the Pharisees to whom the Lord addressed the story of The Rich Man and Lazarus, it is therefore advantageous to acquire a background knowledge of this particular group. The Pharisees were a sect who derived great power and respect among the Jews by virtue of their religious knowledge. Most of the members were laymen, but many were scribes, men who had a higher status due to their formal training in rabbinic law. They lived simply and without the luxuries of their time, a mode of conduct which put them in opposition to the aristocratic Sadducees, (who were very worldly and derived power from their wealth). Pharisees observed and passed on the oral law, or Halakah, which was a tradition of laws pertaining to tithing, fasting, purity, and prayer. The Halakah was purported to have been handed down from Moses, and was given the same high standing as the Pentateuch.

The aim of the Pharisees was to live their everyday lives in the home with the same degree of purity as was practiced in the Temple – and so, to be "a kingdom of priests, and an holy nation" (Exodus 19:6). In their performance of the oral law, they effectively set themselves apart from and above the other Jews. (They lived in their own separate communities.) But they, and their beliefs, carried a tremendous amount of authority, so that eventually all manner of prayer, worship, and sacrifice was performed in harmony with Pharisaic practices. The Lord Himself described them as "sitting in Moses' seat," for in their time they were admired as being the best interpreters of Scripture.

When Jesus Christ began His ministry, He often found Himself in the company of the Pharisees and took them to task repeatedly for their doctrinal errors. Although they were the popular leaders of their people, Christ called them "blind guides," for they were guilty of leading many away from the truth of the Old Testament Scriptures. They had created a system of their own laws, which they adhered to faithfully, but "omitted the weightier matters of the law, judgment, mercy, and faith" (Matthew 23:23). They were also found by the Lord to be making void certain of the commandments of God. (For instance, see Mark 7:1-13 where the Lord criticized the Pharisees misuse of Corban. Some of them were apparently giving away their money as a gift dedicated to God so that they could subsequently avoid the burden of supporting their elderly parents.)

The Pharisaic sect was obviously not held in high esteem by Jesus Christ, for He called them "fools," "serpents," "hypocrites," and a "generation of vipers" (Matthew 23). He condemned their use of the oral law to circumvent the law of the Pentateuch, as was evident in the case of their liberal divorce laws. But apparently one of their more serious errors was their attempt to attain righteousness by adhering to their laws of cleanliness, prayer, and tithing. Such a doctrine totally failed to address the real problem of the need for salvation and the cleansing of the heart of man. It is not surprising that the Lord warned his disciples to "beware of the leaven of the Pharisees" (Matthew 16:6), for much of their doctrine was as poison, and led those who followed it far astray.

With these basics in mind, let us now turn our attention to the Lord's story of The Rich Man and Lazarus. This is the main source of today's most popular doctrines concerning the after-death experience, and it is often regarded as a thinly veiled portrait of reality ... (thus, purportedly demonstrating that there is conscious life after death with comfort for the good and torment for the evil.) But it is these very ideas concerning the dead that are so curious here, for they certainly contradict the many earlier scriptural writings that have been brought forth in the body of this study. For example, we remember that concerning the death of man, the psalmist writes,

> His breath goeth forth, he returneth to his earth: in that very day his thoughts perish. (Psalm 146:4)

Yet in Luke 16, the Lord communicates a story in which men are not only thinking, but talking, seeing, thirsting, and feeling. Other prior Scripture agrees with the psalm, calling death "the land of forgetfulness" (Psalm 88:11-12), and stating that "the dead know not anything" (Ecclesiastes 9:5); and yet the dead in the Lord's story appear to have total awareness. We also recall from the Old Testament that "there is no work, nor device, nor knowledge, nor wisdom in *sheol*" (Ecclesiastes 9:10). But, in the story addressed to the Pharisees, the rich man is represented as using knowledge and wisdom to devise a plan by which his brothers might be warned of the torments he was experiencing.

And, aside from contradicting the basic concept that man "shall not be" in death (Job 7:21), it is also interesting to note that The Rich Man and Lazarus attributes bodies - with eyes, fingers, and tongue - to dead men before the day of resurrection takes place. Other Biblical passages convey that the body undergoes "corruption" in *sheol/hades* (Job 17:13-14, Acts 2:31), so it is puzzling to see that Abraham and the rich man possess living functioning bodies that have not been destroyed by the worm. Indeed, their ability to speak is also an enigma, for it surely contradicts the plain meaning of Psalm 115:17, which indicates that the dead are residing in silence:

> The dead praise not the Lord, neither any that go down into silence. (Psalm 115:17)

In light of all the earlier Biblical testimony concerning the nature of death, the soul, and the fate of the unredeemed, we may certainly wonder how we are to properly reconcile such Scriptures with the Lord's story of Luke 16. Should we be explaining away the earlier Scriptures as the ignorant human reasonings of the ancients in order to receive this New Testament story as the truth? Although this is the solution that many have embraced, it is not the only manner in which this perplexing problem may be solved. If we believe that the Old Testament writings on the death state are accurate and trustworthy, then it is logical to question the *purpose* behind the Lord's story. We may ask whether it is really actual doctrine for our learning, or whether it is perhaps something of another nature that is extremely pertinent to His confrontation with the Pharisees. It cannot be without significance that the entire premise of the story of The Rich Man and Lazarus is in total disagreement with the testimony of the Old Testament Scriptures which come before it. It is likely that there is a reason why the Lord utilized such conflicting ideas here, and when the Pharisees are examined more closely, a plausible reason appears.

According to the historian Josephus, who was himself a member of the sect from the age of 19, the Pharisees believed in the immortality of the soul and a conscious intermediate state between death and resurrection. "They ... believe that souls have an immortal vigour in them, and that under the earth there will be rewards and punishments, according as they have lived virtuously or viciously in this life; and the latter are to be detained in an everlasting prison, but that the former shall have power to revive and live again" (*Antiquities of the Jews,* Book XVIII, Chapter 1, 3). Early Jewish writings in the Talmud and the Midrash – the collections of commentaries which form the body of Jewish tradition – also give evidence of these doctrines, for they contain many beliefs (not always scriptural) which were current in the Lord's day. Rabbinical (and strongly Pharisaic) teachings that had been passed from generation to generation orally were written down and preserved, and in these we are able to see clearly some of the same ideas utilized in "The Rich Man and Lazarus."

Regarding the dead, it is asserted in the writings that they are both aware and able to speak. Berakhot, the first tractate of the Talmud of Babylonia, contains a story in which the dead buried in a cemetery are credited with the knowledge that two men walking above them were trailing their show-fringes on the ground (Chapter 3, VI, A-K). Another narrative attributes speech to the dead; it features two spirits talking with one another, tells of a living man who is able to hear them, and closes with the teaching that the dead *do* know what is happening (Chapter 3, VIII)[5]. The doctrine of the time also allowed that pairs of men could be fatefully coupled together during their earthly life and afterward, seeing and conversing with each other after death as the rich man and Lazarus do. The Midrash on Ruth[6] contains a story which bears a notable resemblance to the one told by the Lord in Luke, demonstrating that these kinds of stories were common vehicles for the teaching of doctrine: Two wicked men associate with each other in this world, and one repents and ends up in the company of the righteous in the Hereafter, while the other stands in the company of the wicked. The wicked man sees and cries out to his righteous friend, and then asks the angels for an opportunity to repent and change his fate. The teaching attributes bodies – with eyes and tongues – to the dead before the day of resurrection.

There is also mention in the Talmud of the circumcised dead sitting in Abraham's Bosom[7] a term which is familiar as the one that Jesus Christ incorporated into His story. Abraham much revered, appears repeatedly in the Jewish teachings on afterlife, and those who died were said to be able to communicate with him. In Berakhot (chapter 3, XI), God is said to have told Moses to *go and tell* Abraham, Isaac, and Jacob that the oath He too to them had been carried out for their children. Similarly, in the Midrash on

---

[5] See Berakhot, *The Talmud of Babylonia,* translated by Jacob Neusner, Brown University, 1984 (pages 138-141).

[6] Ruth Rabbah, Chapter III, 3. See *Midrash Rabbah, Ruth,* translated by Rabbi Dr. L. Rabinowitz, Soncino Press, London/New York, 1983 (page 44).

[7] Qiddushin, Chapter 4, V.42, A. See *The Talmud of Babylonia,* translated by Jacob Neusner, Brown Judaic Studies, Scholars Press, Atlanta, Georgia, 1992 (page 132).

Lamentations[8], there is an account of Miriam, the daughter of Tanhum: When her last son of seven is about to be slain on the same day, she tells the boy to *go to* Abraham and inform the patriarch that his mother had built seven altars and offered up seven sons in a day, (thus calling on Abraham not to be prideful about his righteousness, in that while the offering of Isaac was but a test, the offering of her sons was in earnest). Abraham was obviously believed to be alive and well in an afterlife, and able to be seen, approached, and spoken to by the dead.

It is also interesting to note that in the Midrash on Exodus[9], the wicked are said to be rich and enjoy comfortable living in this world, whereas the righteousness are said to be poor; retribution is promised in the Hereafter, where the wicked will suffer and the righteous will receive the treasures of Eden. And lastly, as to the mode of punishment in "the afterlife," the Midrash on Ecclesiastes[10] contains a statement which very well sums up the numerous references to fire throughout all the writings: The Holy One is quoted as having declared to man that His habitation is pure, His attendants are pure, and the soul given to man is pure. If man returns the soul to God pure, then all is well; but if not, it will be burned. Hence, these were the popular beliefs of the day, and their elements are strikingly similar to various elements used by the Lord in His story to the Pharisees in Luke 16.

Now when we recognize that concepts like "Abraham's Bosom" and consciousness after death were established traditions of these Jews in the New Testament times, the close parallels suggest that Jesus Christ was simply echoing their tradition when He spoke to them that day - and echoing for a specific purpose. When we are aware of the Pharisees' detailed views concerning (what they called) "The Hereafter," and the contradiction of such ideas by the Old Testament Scriptures, it becomes somewhat easier to perceive the Rich Man and Lazarus as something more strategic than it initially appears. The Lord did not actually promulgate eternal existence and conscious punishment in a plain, straightforward, or formal manner here. Rather, He only used them within a cryptic story, or parable, and He did not proceed to explain the story, thereby establishing its basis in fact. This ambiguity allows doubt as to whether the Rich Man and Lazarus was truly intended to depict an after-death reality ... but more importantly, it also permits us to view the story as the

---

[8] Lamentations Rabbah, Chapter I, 16, 50. See *Midrash Rabbah, Lamentations,* translated by Rev. Dr. A. Cohen, Soncino Press, London/New York, 1983 (pages 130-133).

[9] Exodus Rabbah, Chapter XXXI, 5. See *Midrash Rabbah, Exodus*, translated by Rabbi Dr. S.M. Lehrman, Soncino Press, London/New York, 1983, (pages 382-383).

[10] Ecclesiastes Rabbah, Chapter XII, 7, I. See *Midrash Rabbah, Ecclesiastes,* translated by Rev. Dr. A. Cohen, Soncino Press, London/New York, 1983, (page 303).

Lord's very artful and deliberate method of indicting the Pharisees with their own erroneous beliefs.

Going back to the text, we have seen that when members of the sect derided the Lord in Luke 16:14, He responded to their ridicule with a sharp condemnation of their self-righteousness. In a move which was intended to "put them in their place" on more than one count, He rapidly changed subjects and condemned them a second time for their doctrine on divorce. Then, following that, the Lord changed the subject yet again and began a third condemnation of the Pharisees, this time in regard to their doctrine concerning the dead. He phrased His indictment as a story involving the fictional characters of the rich man and Lazarus, resourcefully working in all the false components of Pharisaic teaching. Jesus Christ, then, was already in the midst of condemning these men for erroneous practices when He began to utter His tale; He merely continued His attack by the use of a clever maneuver that was intended to further accuse those Pharisees who were listening that day.

And so, after being derided for The Unjust Steward and His comments that followed, the Lord came back at these men with an ironic story that would expose the leaven of the Pharisees to all in attendance. That Jesus Christ was capable of such irony is demonstrated by His sarcastic remark after The Unjust Steward was completed: "Make to yourselves friends of the mammon of unrighteousness; that, when ye fail, they may receive you into everlasting habitations." These words were not intended as actual advice, and neither was His story to the Pharisees intended as actual instruction for His disciples that day. Both are admirable examples of the Lord's skill in the use of words and language, while The Rich Man and Lazarus had the particular design of a shrewd parody of the Pharisaic beliefs. So here we find a plausible reason why Jesus Christ might tell a story which so contradicts much of the rest of the Scriptures. Those who listened to the Lord in His own day were doubtless aware of the distinctive Pharisaic doctrine, and therefore recognized His cutting irony toward the "vipers" who sat "in Moses' seat."

And indeed, sectarianism within Judaism reveals that not all of the Jews were in agreement as to how the Holy Scriptures were to be understood. All three of the major sects of Christ's time departed from the Scriptures as differences arose regarding numerous aspects of the law, worship, and doctrine. The Sadducees did not believe in resurrection or eternal life of any kind - and therefore did not favor the concept of an immortal soul; their doctrine revolved around all that the Jew had and could do in "this life," rather than a future one. The Essenes and the Pharisees, however both favored the immortality of the soul and a belief that had grown and undergone development among the Jews during the inter-testamental period. Most unfortunate, however, is the strong likelihood that the true origin of the belief came in part from the immensely popular teachings of the Greek philosopher Plato (428/7-348/7 B.C.). In Plato's writings can be found many dramatic ideas of inherent immortality, but in the Bible itself the words "immortal" and "soul" are never put together in order to describe mankind. In the end, one has only to look back to the Jewish and Greek converts to the early church in order to understand how the doctrine of the immortal soul entered into the Christian faith.

In addition to being in sharp disagreement with the rest of the Scriptures on the subject of the death state, The Rich Man and Lazarus also contains other aberrations which tend to flag it as a condemnation of the Pharisees, rather than as a warning of their possible future fate in hell. According to the story, judgment of persons is obviously given immediately upon death, and then torments are applied without delay. (For in order to determine which side of the gulf each soul should be sent to, and who is worthy of "comfort" and "torments," judgment would have to be executed first in order to make such an assessment.) But other portions of Scripture repeatedly teach that there is to be a *future* "day of judgment" (1 John 4:17, 2 Peter 3:7), and this is surely to be after resurrection, as Revelation 20:4 and 20:12 describe. It is also notable that the idea of punishment before the day of judgment is not mentioned in other (more straightforward) Scripture, and in fact, the opposite is true: "The Lord knoweth how ... to reserve the unjust unto the day of judgment to be punished" (2 Peter 2:9). Discrepancies such as these tend to confirm the likelihood that the Lord was using the Pharisees beliefs to make His condemnation of them more biting, for such teachings of immediate "rewards and punishments" "under the earth" were certainly theirs (Josephus, *Antiquities of the Jews*, Book XVIII, Chapter 1, 3.)

And faith is an issue here, as well, because if the Rich Man and Lazarus truly teaches a factual scenario for man, then it also appears to oppose all that the Lord Jesus Christ has said about faith as the basis of salvation (see Chapter 5, Faith is the Key to Eternal Life). The Apostle Paul has shown us in Romans 5:17 that "they which receive abundance of grace and of the gift of righteousness shall reign in life," and chapter four is clear that righteousness is received by faith ... not by works. The Lord's story to the Pharisees, on the other hand, shows us a poor man and a rich man, and the implied reason that the poor man is "comforted" after death in Abraham's bosom is that he suffered a life of poverty (Luke 16:25); nothing is said about whether he was a God fearing man of faith or not. Likewise, the rich man seems to suffer torments because he neglected to give aid to the poor man. He failed to do a good work, but again, there is no mention about whether or not he was a man who had faith in God. Thus , according to the story, reward or suffering after death seems to be directly related to circumstances other than faith. Lazarus is rewarded because he suffered on earth, where people apparently failed to do good works towards him; and the rich man failed to provide for his brother. The traditional teaching in Exodus Rabbah – that the wicked are rich and the righteous are poor – seems to be paralleled here, and this again suggests that the Lord was using the Pharisees' own beliefs in His story. Faith appears to be a non-existent issue, leaving us to question whether this scenario, and this story, are even loosely based on the facts of Scripture.

Finally, it is interesting to note that both Pharisaic traditions, and the story that the Lord directed at the Pharisees, describe a happy afterlife of "comfort" in the Hereafter for the redeemed (be they poor or otherwise). According to tradition, the dead would go to Abraham, to sit pleasantly in his "bosom" and enjoy the blessings of righteousness, while fiery torments were applied to the wicked. But, if *sheol/hades* is truly a spiritual realm where the people of God were once housed prior to the ascension of Christ, it is questionable what kind of comfort they actually would have experienced there if they were made to reside in plain view of the unsaved. Many would consider this a *dis*comforting situation, and one that would have been mentally torturous for the saintly as well as the unredeemed. As the Lord's story illustrates, unsaved family and friends would have undergone a terrorizing suffering within visible distance and earshot of the saved, and would have called out continually for merciful favors and relief. If this – or anything like it - is what God has elsewhere referred to as the "sleep" of death (Deuteronomy 31:16, John 11:11), then such slumber must have been characterized by a nightmare of the most horrible magnitude for the early peoples of God. It may indeed be no coincidence that the term "Abraham's Bosom" occurs only once in the entire Bible, and this while the Lord is actively engaged in a criticism of Israel's "blind guides." This view of an afterlife belongs to the tradition of men, as the early uninspired Jewish writings are able to demonstrate.

On many points, then, the Rich Man and Lazarus strays from the teaching of the rest of Scriptures: the death state, the nature of soul and spirit, the nature of *sheol/hades,* the fate of the unredeemed. The story speaks of the possession of bodies before resurrection; of judgment and punishment before judgment day; of salvation by works. The fact that it deviates so greatly from the body of Scripture surrounding it should be a testimony in itself that it is not teaching, but false doctrine held up to the faces of those searching for the truth will find confidence when they begin to embrace all of the teachings of the Bible – both Old Testament and New Testament, from beginning to end.

Because of its apparent relationship to, and condemnation of, Pharisaic doctrine, some have hesitated to call The Rich Man and Lazarus a parable, although it does not fit the bill in some respects. It is a story with characters and events, and although its meaning is not explained by the Lord in Scripture, it unquestionably appears to be teaching a lesson. Coming as it does, after the parable of the Unjust Steward and after the Lord's direct criticism of the Pharisees, it seems to give an example of how the Pharisees themselves were unjust stewards – not with material goods, but with the word of God, which had been entrusted to them as the spiritual leaders of their people. That the Pharisees had not been wholly faithful to God's word is evident by the Scriptures, and their doctrine concerning the death state was the Lord's case in point. His inclusion of prophetic note makes it all the more interesting: for when a real Lazarus would rise from the dead some time later, the event would fail to persuade the nation of the authenticity of Jesus Christ, just as

"Abraham" predicted that the raising of the fictional Lazarus would not convince the rich man's brothers.

When the Lord finished His address to the Pharisees in Luke 16:31, He turned to His disciples again and said, "It is impossible but that offences will come; but woe unto him, through whom they come! It were better for him that a millstone were hanged about his neck, and he cast into the sea, than that he should offend one of these little ones" (17:1-2). Thus, after condemning the Pharisees with their own beliefs, He tells the disciples that it is better to be dead than to be found guilty of placing doctrinal stumbling blocks in front of other people. These are harsh words, but they demonstrate to us how strongly God feels about those who teach from the wisdom of oral tradition which contradicts the word of God.[11]

---

[11] For me on this subject see *The Rich Man and Lazarus* by E W Bullinger published both as a book, by the Open Bible Trust, and as an eBook by Amazon and Apple. See page 144 for more details.

Appendix 2: Problematic Scriptures.

The verses given below are an occasional source of difficulty for the student of the Scriptures. To some eyes they may seem to support the popular traditional doctrines, while to others they may not. Listed below are passages that have not been fully considered within the body of this study; they are analyzed with the principle of conditional immortality in view.

Genesis 35:18 ...

may seem to indicate that an "eternal soul" departs the body at death. What is leaving Rachel in this verse is *nephesh*, her life ..." for she died." The verse does not specifically state that the soul is eternal, but only mentions that it was departing.

Deuteronomy 32:22 ...

may seem to indicate that there is a real hell which burns with fire. This occurrence of *sheol* is contained within the "Song of Moses," and the context at this point (read to verse 25) is God's threat of judgment on Israel with the tribulation to come (cp. Revelation 15:3-5). The judgment fire is used with regard to physical sufferings here on earth: hunger, heat (possibly volcanic, noting reference to mountains), death, beasts, and swords. There is the possibility of actual fire raining down from God as in O.T. times (see Revelation 8:7-11, 9:17-18, 11:5, 16:8-9, 18:8-10). The Lord's fire which shall "burn unto the lowest grave" is a figurative method of implying that no one can escape from the wrath to come; His fire of judgment will search the entire earth. The verse does not contain enough information to establish *sheol* as a spiritual realm, but only confirms that it is a place of some depth.

1 Samuel 28:3-20 ...

may seem to indicate that Samuel was a living spirit/disembodied soul after his death. The passage speaks of "bringing him up" through a "familiar spirit" (verse 8), and of "seeing" the dead Samuel as "an old man ... covered with a mantle" (verses 13,14). The most noteworthy thing about this passage is that Saul never saw Samuel; as in today's séances, the medium told him what she saw, and when the dead Samuel "spoke" he spoke through the medium. The woman with the familiar spirit claimed to see "an old man ... covered with a mantle," but if this was actually Samuel, where did his disembodied soul get a body? Did God perform a resurrection of Samuel at the request of this woman? Or did she herself have the power to force even the faithful dead to return to the earth in order to speak? If we believe that the dead "go down into silence" as Psalm 115:17 indicates, then we understand why Saul was committing a serious transgression when he sought out a woman with a "familiar spirit." Such "mediums" do not contact the living spirits of dead men, but demonic spirits who speak through them and impersonate the dead. The practice was as ungodly as the worship of idols, and those with familiar spirits were to be put to death (Leviticus 20:27). People with familiar spirits were also said to be defiling to the one who made use of them (Leviticus 19:31). This would seem odd if the "user" was merely attempting communication with a deceased human - especially one of God's faithful - but very consistent if one was conversing with demons. Thus the penalty was death and the practice was condemned. 1 Chronicles 10:13-14 states that "Saul died," in part for asking counsel of one that had a familiar spirit, to enquire of it." See Deuteronomy 18:10-12.

1 Kings 17:17-23 ...

may seem to indicate that an "eternal soul" departs the body at death and returns again at resurrection. This occurrence of *nephesh* can be understood as the *life* of the child returning to his body, and so, reviving him. The resurrection is identical to the miracle that the Lord performed on Lazarus in John 11:1-44. The passage does not state that *nephesh* is an eternal entity, but only says that it "came into him again" - just as life would come in again to anyone who is truly redeemed from the state of death.

Job 32:8 ...

may seem to indicate that man possesses an "eternal spirit." Elihu states that "there is a *ruach* in man," and in this instance he is most likely referring to the "*ruach* of life" from God (Psalm 104:30). The verse does not state that the spirit in man is an eternal one that constitutes the man himself, but only confirms that an animating force of some kind is there.

Psalm 73:24 ...

may seem to indicate that man is "received" into God's presence immediately after death. It is true that God will receive us, but not until the return of the Lord and the time appointed for resurrection (Job 14:3, Job 14:13-15). This verse only declares that man will be received; it does not say that this will happen at death, but simply "afterward," which can be interpreted as meaning after the return and resurrection have taken place.

Proverbs 23:13-14 ...

may seem to indicate that the wicked will "go to hell." In this occurrence of both *nephesh* and *sheol*, *nephesh* is used as a pronoun, so that the last verse may be read as, "deliver him from the grave." The proverb stresses the importance of instilling proper values and behavior in a child, so as to prevent transgressions which could ultimately result in the loss of his life. It is probable that capital punishment is alluded to here, but the loss may be a more eternal one, as well.

Ecclesiastes 3:21 ...

may seem to indicate that man possesses an "eternal spirit" that departs the body at death. As the verse appears in the *KJV*, the reader is left with the impression that the spirits of men and beasts go in different directions at death - and thus, to different places. But, using the Masoretic Text, *Green's Interlinear Hebrew/Greek English Bible* has rendered the verse, "Who knows the spirit of the sons of man (if) it goes upward, and the spirit of the beast (if) it goes downward to the earth?" With this translation, we see the destination of the spirit questioned rhetorically, rather than stated definitively. The answer called for is that no one knows, but some clarification may be gleaned from the preceding verse 19. There it is stated that man and beast have "one breath," or *ruach*/spirit, "so that a man hath no preeminence above a beast." Thus, there is nothing different or special about the spirit that resides in mankind, for both he and the beast receive God's life-giving *ruach* simply in order to live. A few chapters later in Ecclesiastes 12:7, it is said that "the spirit shall return unto God Who gave it." If man and beast truly have one *ruach* that is identical in both, then it stands to reason that in both cases the spirit shall return to the Giver of life - for He is "the God of the spirits of all flesh" (Numbers 27:16). None of these passages specifically state that the human spirit being spoken of is an eternal one that forms an integral part of man's personal being; nor is it actually confirmed that the spirits of man and beast go to different places after death.

Isaiah 8:19 ...

may seem to indicate that the dead are living and can be sought through familiar spirits. The question is poorly phrased in the *KJV,* and is rendered by *Green's Interlinear Bible* as, "Should not a people seek to its God, than for the living to seek to the dead?" The question is a rhetorical one, and the answer is emphatically yes. The verse does not state that the dead are alive, but only suggests that there is no profit in seeking them. This rings true when we remember that the dead are "sleeping."

Isaiah 55:3 ...

may seem to indicate that the faithful have an "eternal soul" which will have life with God - (a scenario which is usually set in contrast to the traditional "spiritual death" in hell experienced by the "eternal soul" of the godless). This verse declares that the godly *nephesh* will live; there is the implication that the godless man will not live, but this absence of life is not specifically explained to be a "spiritual death" in hellfire. The verse does not state that the soul is eternal in nature, and only the covenant is said to be "everlasting."

Isaiah 59:1-2 ...

may seem to indicate that the "immortal souls" of unsaved men will be forever separated from God within an eternal hell. (For it is traditionally held that all men have "immortal souls," and thus the unatoned sinner must consciously experience the separation caused by his sin for all of eternity.) This passage simply states that sin has caused a separation between man and his God. The remedy is, of course, Jesus Christ, but its alternative is not explicitly stated within the verses. The passage cannot establish that separation from God entails "spiritual death" in an eternally separate hell of fire.

Ezekiel 32:17-28 ...

may seem to indicate that the dead are alive and able to speak within *sheol.* While the dead are said to speak "out of the midst of *sheol*" in verse 21, they are also said to have "gone down to *sheol* with their weapons of war" in verse 27, and it is implied that they are buried there with "their swords under their heads." This suggests very strongly that *sheol* was intended as "the grave" in this prophecy, and that personification was used when the dead were given voice. Take note of the surrounding context in which the words "pit" (verses 18, 24) and "graves" (verses 22, 23, 25, 26) occur repeatedly; these are *bor* and *keber*, both of which describe burial places, and which help to establish the sense in which we should understand *sheol*. Lastly, Psalm 94:17 and Job 3:11-19 would both seem to disallow the possibility of speech while in the death state.

Jonah 1:15-2:10 ...

may seem to indicate that the dead are alive and able to speak within *sheol* - (for Jonah writes that he cried "out of the belly of hell.") If we allow that Jonah was still alive in the water when the fish advanced on him and opened it's mouth to devour him, then we may also allow that Jonah may easily have been alive in the belly of the fish for a short time before losing consciousness. Even ten seconds is time enough for a quick thinking man to pray for deliverance, and his "crying out" may just as well have been executed from the heart, as from the mouth. In this way, Jonah could have prayed "out of the belly of *sheol*" without necessarily being alive and conscious beyond his death; he was merely praying from within the fish that he knew would soon become his grave. Jonah is, of course, a type of the death, burial, and resurrection of Jesus Christ, having died within the fish and then being quickened again just prior to (or upon) being vomited out. Jonah, like Christ, was dead in *sheol*, and both had their lives "brought up" from the "corruption" that takes place there; Jonah 2:6, Acts 2:31.) The prayer of Jonah was written down after his ordeal had taken place and in 2:7 he says that "When my soul fainted within me I remembered the Lord: and my prayer came in unto Thee." This then, would seem to be the actual moment of his prayer from *sheol* – the last seconds of consciousness when his life was fainting away.

Zechariah 12:1 ...

may seem to indicate that man possesses an "eternal spirit." In this verse, which identifies the Lord by His mighty works, we are told that God formed the *ruach* within man. Very likely a reference to Genesis 2:7, the verse only confirms that there is a spirit of some kind within man, and that God formed it. It does not state that the spirit is eternal in nature, and there is no implication that it can exist as a personal entity independently of the body.

Matthew 8:11-12 ...

may seem to indicate that there will be eternal conscious punishment of the wicked. This passage is spoken to the Gentile centurion who showed great faith. He and others outside Israel ("many ... from the east and west") will share the kingdom of heaven, while those to whom it was offered (Israel, "the children of the kingdom") will be cast into the outer darkness. The Lord is discussing faith and reward, and so end-time judgment is in view; but there is nothing to indicate that we should equate being "cast into outer darkness" with a fate in an eternal hell of fire. The context seems to compare the tremendous faith of one, the centurion, with the lesser (or non-existent) faith within the chosen nation: "I have not found so great faith, no, not in Israel." Some, therefore, see the Lord as speaking about rewards given for various degrees of faith, with "the outer darkness" representing an eternal position in the kingdom which is outside the very center of things. (With many thousands of people present, not everyone can sit next to Abraham, Isaac, and Jacob; faith might determine the seating order, with some seated far away from the place of honor.) Others interpret the Lord's words about "outer darkness" differently, and see them as pertaining to the more severe judgment of those unsaved Jews who remain on the earth at His return. In this view, being cast out into outer darkness is viewed as synonymous with destruction in *Gehenna,* so that the Lord is seen to be discussing judgment of life or death here, rather than degrees of faith. The passage is a difficult one, for the Lord does not explain his words in detail. But whatever the case may be, it is apparent that those put into outer darkness will weep when judgment is pronounced, and mental anguish is in view on the occasion, as well. Again there is no indication that these people might experience eternal conscious punishment in an eternal hell of fire, for no such place is specifically mentioned. See also Luke 13:24-30.

Matthew 17:1-9 ...

may seem to indicate that Moses and Elijah are alive beyond the grave. This incident was not an actual sighting of these two men, but a vision of the same nature that Peter was shown in Acts 11:5-10; the same Greek word (*horama*) is used to describe both experiences, in Matthew 17:9 and Acts 11:5 respectively. Many Scriptures have already been given in this study that demonstrate that an actual presence of Moses and Elijah is not possible, for both are dead and "sleeping." Furthermore, it is obvious that bodies were seen, because Christ is said to be observed talking to the men. If this was not a vision, what bodies would these be? ... the resurrection of the saints has yet to occur. Also bear in mind that Christ was yet to be the firstfruits of those that sleep (1 Corinthians 15:22-23); He was to be the first to be clothed with a heavenly body, and no others could precede Him. (See also Acts 16:9 and 18:9 where *horama*, meaning "that which is seen," obviously describes two other visions.)

Matthew 22:23-33 ...

may seem to indicate that the dead are not really dead - (due to the presence of the Lord's words,"God is not the God of the dead, but of the living.") The Sadducees' question about resurrection (verses 24-28) was asked in mockery, and Jesus Christ's answer was formed specifically to defend the doctrine as the truth. By proclaiming that God is the God of the living, He asserted that the resurrection is indeed a reality - that the dead would not *remain* dead, but would rise again to life. Therefore, God is (even now) the God of Abraham not because Abraham is yet alive somewhere, but because he will certainly rise from the dead. It was this clever saying that caused His audience to be "astonished," for the Lord was contending that Abraham, Isaac, and Jacob must be resurrected in order to continue in life with their God. (If the fathers are "living" even now, as some say Christ is contending here, how does this prove that the resurrection is a reality?) The passage does not state that the dead are actually living somewhere, but it does strongly imply that resurrection is the means by which they will one day be given their promised life. (See also Mark 12:18-27, Luke 20:27-38.)

Matthew 25:31-46 ...

may seem to indicate that there will be eternal conscious punishment of the wicked. The term "everlasting punishment" only occurs once in the Bible, on this single occasion (verse 46) in the New Testament. At the end-time gathering of the nations, the Lord will separate the sheep from the goats: the blessed will inherit the kingdom, but the cursed are to "depart ... into everlasting fire," going away into "everlasting punishment." This "everlasting" punishment is the Lord's own capital punishment which He repeatedly symbolized with the use of *Gehenna* - an execution of flesh and blood which is irreversible and age-abiding. The manner of this death is by fire, which God will use to destroy the body and soul forever (as the disciples are forewarned in Matthew 10:28). Thus, the punishment spoken of here is essentially the same punishment promised in Romans 6:23: "the wages of sin is death." But in this instance it is emphasized with dramatic finality, and with the "foreverness" implying that there is no subsequent chance of life. The flames that burn forever are given to convey the fact that the destruction of the unredeemed will also last for all time - the flames will never stop burning, and never cease so that a moment for resurrection might occur. The verses do not state that there is eternal *conscious* punishment for the unsaved; they only state that some men will depart into an everlasting fire, and that the punishment inflicted thereby will also be everlasting. There is no indication that the men themselves will last forever, or that the fire will fail to consume and destroy them.

Luke 1:46-47 ...

may seem to indicate that man possesses an "eternal soul" and an "eternal spirit." In these verses, both *psuche* and *pneuma* are used figuratively in place of ordinary pronouns in order to emphasize Mary's exceedingly great joy. Words which ordinary represent life, and the invisible spark which bestows it, are instead given to represent the self by the figure synecdoche (where a part of something is put for the whole of it). The passage confirms that Mary possessed both *psuche* and *pneuma*, but it does not state plainly that either is eternal.

Luke 8:49-55 ...

may seem to indicate that man has an "eternal spirit" that departs the body at death and returns at resurrection. This occurrence of *pneuma* can be understood as the life-giving spirit from God returning to the maiden's body, and so, restoring her life (see Revelation 11:11). The verse does not state that this spirit was an eternal one that constituted the maiden herself, but only says that it "came again" to her - just as the breath of life would come again to anyone who is truly revived from death.

Luke 23:43 ...

may seem to indicate that man has an "eternal soul/spirit" that will go to paradise immediately upon death. Many are unaware that early manuscripts of the New Testament are totally without punctuation as we know it today, and such marks do not appear on any manuscripts until the ninth century. This means that the original Scriptures were not punctuated, and what we see in our Bible today has been added exclusively by man according to his own judgment. The bias of the translators obviously led them to place the comma where they did, but the verse may just as well be rendered, "Verily I say unto thee this day, with Me thou shalt be in the paradise." This translation is justified by, a)the probable use of the Hebrew idiom, "I say unto thee *this day*," which is used 42 times for solemn emphasis throughout Deuteronomy (4:40, 8:19, 11:2, 26, 30:11, 32:46, and also Acts 26:2); and b),the presence of the article before "paradise," making it "the paradise." This is most likely the paradise (containing the tree of life) that is to be restored in Revelation 22, and so this paradise is not yet accessible (see Genesis 3:24). It is also interesting to note that the Lord *would not be able* to be in paradise with the malefactor "today," for He was constrained to spend the next three days and nights in *sheol/hades* utterly dead (Matthew 12:40, Acts 2:31). After His resurrection He told Mary Magdalene that He had not yet ascended to His Father (John 20:17), and so it is doubtful that He and the malefactor had already been to a heavenly paradise. Finally, it is also of benefit to consider the malefactor's dying request to be "remembered" *when Jesus Christ comes into His kingdom* (Luke 23:42). This event was not to take place "today," (upon Christ's death), but is even now still future. Thus the malefactor's words strongly suggest that his sole hope toward Christ was to be remembered and "raised up at the last day" when the King returns in glory.

Romans 2:6-11 …

may seem to indicate that there will be eternal conscious torment in hellfire for the unredeemed. The threat of "indignation and wrath, tribulation and anguish, upon every soul of man that doeth evil" is ominous indeed, but it does not necessarily imply eternal conscious punishment. "Tribulation and anguish' may be seen as referring to the mental distress or suffering that may take place at judgment, or even prior to execution. (For some, the judgment or works may be quite an ordeal, so that these words may accurately describe the anguish in their minds, rather than an agony brought about the experience of physical pain.) Also, while it may seem to some readers that "immortal souls" will meet with the tribulation described, the figurative use of *psuche* should be recognized here so that the threat is seen to be upon "every man" or "every person" that "doeth evil"... not upon every never-dying soul. As the verses do not mention "*eternal* tribulation and anguish," or "every *immortal* soul," it would be impossible to say that a never-ending "hell" is the interpretation that God intended here. Verse 7, however, does state that "eternal life" is to be rendered to those who seek glory, honor, and immortality, so that the only mention of eternal existence in this passage is in reference to the gift of everlasting life.

1 Corinthians 2:10-12 ...

may seem to indicate that man possesses an "eternal spirit." Paraphrased, the meaning of this passage is that man can know the deep things of himself, of his own mind, and the things of his world, but he cannot know the things of God unless he receives the "spirit which is of God." (This would not be the spirit of life which animates the body, but the spirit of Christ which makes man alive unto God.) Verse 14 emphasizes that the natural/*psuchikos*/soulish man (who "abides in death") cannot receive God's wisdom, but only the spiritual man, i.e., those born of the spirit. When we have this new spiritual nature residing within us, it can then be said that "we have the mind of Christ" (verse 16). The verses do not state or imply that "the spirit of man" is eternal in nature, but only maintain that man, of his own spirit or self, can never perceive the spiritual things of God.

2 Corinthians 5:1-10 ...

may seem to indicate that a faithful man will be present with the Lord immediately upon his death. [It is important to remember that at the time 2 Corinthians was written, the kingdom was being re-offered to Israel by the apostles, and was therefore still "at hand." Thus, the church in existence at that time was living in the expectation of the imminent return of the Lord, and therefore hoped to be transformed, or "changed," rather than see death (1 Corinthians 15:51). This passage from 2 Corinthians - and all others penned between the Ascension and the postponement of the kingdom at Acts 28:28 - should be read with this hope in mind.] Paul's earnest desire in these verses was to be clothed upon with the "house which is from heaven," the promised spiritual body that is fitted for eternity. He hoped to be transformed from his earthly body into his heavenly body, and thus avoid "being found naked." This naked, or "unclothed," state is the state of death, in which Paul would have neither the earthly house nor the house from heaven - and it was obviously not desired (verses 3-4). The apostle did not wish to sleep, or die, but he hoped to remain alive until the second coming of the Lord; and then, to be "changed," as "in the twinkling of an eye" (1 Corinthians 15:51-52), into his new spiritual body, and so avoid the sting of death. He referred to this "change" or transformation as being "clothed upon, that mortality might be swallowed up of life." And because of his great confidence in this promise of God's, he was ready and willing "to be absent from the body, *and* to be present with the Lord." He longed for ("groaned" for) the return of Jesus Christ and the transformed heavenly body that would be his at that very moment.

But "whether present or absent," he labored and sought to be pleasing to Him, knowing that when his earthly house was "dissolved" (or "changed") into the spiritual "house which is from heaven," judgment would follow soon after. While this passage does not specifically state that man will be with the Lord immediately upon death, it does inform us that Paul *desired* to be absent from his earthly body, and present with the Lord in a new body fitted for eternity.

Philippians 1:18-25 ...

may seem to indicate that a faithful man will be present with the Lord immediately upon his death. [This passage is similar to 2 Corinthians 5:1-10 above, but the kingdom was now in abeyance and death, rather than a transforming "change", was expected for the saints. Once Israel was temporarily set aside due to their unbelief, (Acts 28:28), it was then known that the Lord would not return to set up His kingdom imminently, but that a considerable time might pass in which the Gentiles would be called. The possibility of remaining alive until the return of Christ was vanquished, passed on to another group of faithful that we now know would live many hundreds of years future to the apostles and their flocks. Thus Paul speaks in Phillipians of the choice of living or dying, but no longer mentions the hope of remaining alive until the "change"] of translation.] Paul was desirous of being with the Lord and expressed that whether he lived or died, Christ would be magnified in his body. He then elaborated, stating that "to live is Christ, and to die is gain." But there appears to be a double ellipsis here, for the former verse indicates that Christ would be served in either case. (Thus, Paul's death would not be Paul's gain, but Christ's.) Read therefore, "For to me to live is Christ's gain, and to die is Christ's gain. But if I live in the flesh, this (Christ's gain) is the fruit of my labor." While it was more fruitful for others if Paul remained alive, death might have seemed a blessing to this man who was in prison, and he did confess that he was "in a strait betwixt" the two. His heart's desire was to depart from life, and to be with Christ, which would be "far better" than his life in prison. But the mere act of departing from life does not necessarily imply that a presence before Christ would immediately take place. (A more contemporary Scripture from Paul's own hand states that the Lord is "dwelling in the light which no man can approach unto; Whom no man hath seen, nor can see," 1 Timothy 6:16.) Other Scriptures suggest that there would be a time spent within the grave (Job 14:12-14), and a recognition of this period does not conflict with Paul's "desire to depart, and to be with Christ." Such words might easily be spoken by any man who expects to fall asleep in death (depart), and then wake up some time later (be with Christ). And, since there is no awareness of the passage of time during "sleep," death could be (and should be) perceived as a doorway to resurrection and God's presence. The verses do not explicitly state that Paul would be with the Lord as a soul/spirit immediately upon his death, but simply outline this man's simple longing to die and be with his Lord.

1 Thessalonians 5:23 ...

may seem to indicate that man is born as a trinity of mortal body, "immortal soul," and "immortal spirit." This benediction closing an epistle expresses the hope that the Thessalonians would be preserved whole, and thus alive, until the coming of the Lord. With the kingdom "at hand," the apostle prayed that they would "be alive and remain" (4:17), rather than have the *psuche* and *pneuma* depart the body in death. In using the words "spirit and soul and body," Paul is simply mentioning three very vital aspects of a living person: perhaps *the* most vital aspects. But he does not specifically state that any of these aspects are eternal in nature, or that any of them alone comprises a person's "eternal being." It should be noted that God has referred to man's composition as such: "...dust thou art, and unto dust shalt thou return" (Genesis 3:19). Accordingly, Abraham came before the Lord describing himself as "but dust and ashes" (Genesis 18:27), implying that he consisted of only these lowly elements, and no more.

Hebrews 11:5 ...

may seem to indicate that Enoch, through "translation," received a spiritual body and eternal life long before the Lord Jesus Christ did. While this verse reveals that God "translated" Enoch" that he should not see death," there are no words to indicate that he was taken to the heavenly sphere. (Genesis 5:24 does not say where God put him after he "took" him; Hebrews 11:5 states merely that Enoch "was not found." And John 3:13 also states quite clearly that "No man hath ascended up to heaven, but he that came down from heaven, even the Son of man which is in heaven.") The Apostle Paul also remains silent as to exactly what happened, or whether any transformation took place, but his words in 1 Timothy 6:16 do at least inform us that Enoch cannot now be with the Lord Jesus Christ. Some readers may be accustomed to equating this "translation" with the transforming "change" that will befall the living saints upon the return of the Lord, thus granting Enoch a new spiritual body at the time he was "taken." In this respect, it is interesting to know that the Greek word translated as "translated" is *metatithemi*, and while it occurs (only) in Acts 7:16 ("carried over"), Galatians 1:6 ("removed"), Hebrews 7:12 ("changed"), Hebrews 11:5 ("translated"), and Jude 4 ("turning"), the word was not used by Paul in describing the "change" (*allasso*, 1 Corinthians 15:51) that will occur when "mortality is swallowed up of life" (2 Corinthians 5:4). But much more importantly, because the Son of God is said to have "the preeminence" in all things (Colossians 1:18), it seems highly unlikely that Enoch could have received an immortal spiritual body fitted for eternity before the Lord Himself did ... and before the Lord actually defeated sin and death via His own death and resurrection. Thus, some have suggested that Enoch was "removed" or "carried over" out of the earthly sphere, and that his life was (or has been) sustained until the proper season for his transformation. Others, on the other hand, believe that Enoch eventually did die, pointing to his inclusion in the list of persons of whom it is said, "these all died in faith" (Hebrews 11:13). This latter view suggests that God "took" Enoch and gently sent him to sleep Himself, that he would not see death in the usual (and perhaps painful) way. And indeed, the wording of the Scripture is interesting: "and *he was not;* for God took him." (The *NIV* translates, "then *he was no more,* because God took him away.") To some the words merely indicate that Enoch was "not here anymore," while to others they suggest that he was "not existing anymore." Thus, it has been proposed that "not seeing death" may describe an exemption from the conscious experience of dying, but not necessarily an exemption from the state of being dead. In this instance, Paul's mention of "translation" would be seen as an easy and compassionate transfer from life to death, rather than a transfer from one sphere to another, or a transformation from a mortal state to an immortal one. Aside from Enoch, there is also a similar question about the status of Elijah (2 Kings 2:11). While most translations tell us that he "went up by a whirlwind into heaven," *Green's Interlinear Bible* shows us that he "went up ... in a tempest to *the heavens,"* which may merely indicate the sky, or the atmosphere surround the earth. (The word used is *shamayim,* which can describe the sky (Deuteronomy 4:17, "air"), the realm of the celestial bodies (Nehemiah 9:23), or the habitation of God Himself (Deuteronomy 26:15)). Hence, we know for sure that Elijah "went up," but where exactly he went to is difficult to ascertain. (See also Matthew 17:1-9 in this appendix.) Whatever the case may be with these instances, again, it seems very improbable that a transformation to immortality might have occurred for these men prior to the glorification of Jesus Christ.

1 Peter 3:18-20 ...

may seem to indicate that there is a hell containing the ungodly "eternal spirits" of men. This passage speaks of the angels of Genesis 6:1-4, as indicated by its reference to the time of Noah. These "sons of God saw the daughters of men" and took them as wives, thereby creating a race of "giants." But the family of Noah, (who was perfect in his generations and therefore fit for the genealogy of Christ), was preserved from the subsequent global destruction by flood. 2 Peter 2:4-5 also speaks of these "angels that sinned," and likewise makes the connection between them and the old world of Noah. Since angels are truly spirit-beings, they are most likely the "spirits in prison" that are mentioned here. Christ's "preaching" to them is better understood as a "proclamation," which is an acceptable translation of the Greek word *kerusso*. The angelic "spoiling" of the human race is often theorized to have been a Satanic effort to defile the line through which the Saviour would come. It is reasonable, then, that Christ would go to the angels in their prison when His work was completed, announcing His victory as well as their humiliating defeat.

2 Peter 2:4 ...

May seem to indicate that there is an eternal hell. What the *KJV* renders "hell" in this verse, is neither *hades* nor *Gehenna*, but *Tartaroo*. This single occurrence of the word suggests that it is Biblically associated with angels, rather than men. It would not be judicious to speculate any further than to presume that these angels are the "spirits in prison" mentioned in 1 Peter 3:19. (See 1 Peter 3:18-20 above.)

Revelation 6:9-11 ...

may seem to indicate that man remains conscious and alive between death and resurrection (via an "eternal soul"). The figure used to give voice to the martyred souls here is personification, and it is similarly used by God when He confronted Cain with the murder of Abel: "the voice of thy brother's blood crieth unto Me from the ground." We do not actually attribute speech to the blood of Abel, and we are most likely not meant to attribute speech to the "lives" lost for the testimony of Christ. Rather, we can see this passage as representing God's own acknowledgement of the souls being lost (Matthew 16:25), with the implication that He is staying His wrath until "their fellowservants also and their brethren, that should be killed as they were, should be fulfilled." To those who will read Revelation during the coming days of tribulation, these words may be a great comfort in the face of the many *deaths occurring on behalf of the Lord. While this passage may imply "immortality of the soul" to those who wish to find it here, the abundance of surreal images in Revelation enables others to interpret it as just another symbolic scene in John's vision.

Revelation 14:9-11 ...

may seem to indicate that there will be eternal conscious punishment for the unrighteous. The word translated "tormented" (*basanidzo*) in verse 10 is derived from *basanos*, a black rock formerly used as a "touchstone." Ancient peoples were able to determine the purity of gold and silver by observing the peculiar streak left on the stone when rubbed by these metals. *Basanos* came into more general use as a test or trial for determining quality or genuineness, and eventually became connected with "torment" when associated with the cruel methods used in ancient inquisitions. The use of *basanidzo* in this passage suggests a trial or examination by the Son to Whom all judgment is committed; the figure of "fire and brimstone" is once again used to indicate His judgment, as a fire which burns and "searches" thoroughly, and from which nothing can be hidden. (Please note also that the guilty are to be tormented "in the presence of the holy angels" and "in the presence of the Lamb." This suggests a one-time event of shorter duration - a trial with Judge and witnesses - rather than an ongoing and eternal event which would seem to necessitate the constant presence of Jesus Christ in hell.) The use of "the smoke of their torment" in verse 11 is also figurative, and is put for the findings of this trial. Like the smoke of destroyed Babylon (19:3), it is said to rise "for ever and ever," thereby illustrating the permanence of God's judgments which will be "on record" for eternity. Lastly, it is said in verse 11 that those who worship the beast and his image shall have no "rest" day and night. As the days and nights seem to indicate a definite time period rather than an eternity, it is likely that this speaks of the time before their trial by fire, rather than after. This appears to be confirmed by verse 13 in which those who die in the Lord find "rest" from their labors. The rigors of this tribulation period (three and a half years) will make death for the saints the equivalent of a rest break from their testing; but the wicked will be plagued day and night right up to its end. (Revelation 9:6).

Further reading:

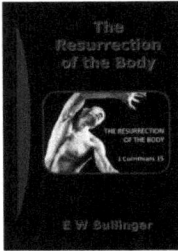

The Resurrection of the Body
E W Bullinger

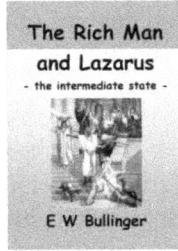

The Rich Man and Lazarus
E W Bullinger

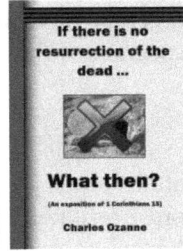

If there is no resurrection of the dead ... what then?
Charles Ozanne

The Life and Soul of Mortal Man
Charles Ozanne

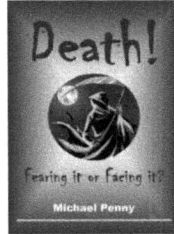

Death! Fearing it or facing it?
Michael Penny

Immortality! When?
Michael Penny

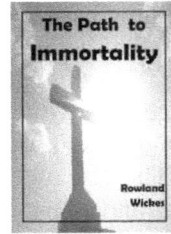

The Path to Immortality
Rowland Wickes

Further details of these books,
and others,
can be seen on **www.obt.org**

They can all be ordered
from that website and also from

The Open Bible Trust
Fordland Mount, Upper Basildon,
Reading, RG8 8LU, UK.

They are also all available as eBooks
from Amazon and Apple
and as KDP paperbacks from Amazon.

About the author

Helaine Burch was born in Queens, NY, USA, and was educated at Bethpage High School and Hunter Business School. An equestrian all of her life, she has been Director of two non-profit Equine Assisted Therapy Programs. At present she lives in Maryland, USA, and is Promotion Head for a yearly music festival in North Carolina, USA.

****

Publications of The Open Bible Trust must be in accordance with its evangelical, fundamental and dispensational basis. However, beyond this minimum, writers are free to express whatever beliefs they may have as their own understanding, provided that the aim in so doing is to further the object of The Open Bible Trust. A copy of the doctrinal basis is available at **www.obt.org.uk/doctrinal-basis** or from:

THE OPEN BIBLE TRUST
Fordland Mount, Upper Basildon,
Reading, RG8 8LU, UK

www.ingramcontent.com/pod-product-compliance
Lightning Source LLC
Chambersburg PA
CBHW071548040426
42452CB00008B/1108